RUSSIAN RELIGIOUS PHILOSOPHY
Selected aspects

RUSSIAN RELIGIOUS PHILOSOPHY

Selected aspects

FREDERICK C. COPLESTON
S.J., F.B.A.

Professor Emeritus of
History of Philosophy in the
University of London

SEARCH PRESS
UNIVERSITY OF NOTRE DAME

Search Press Ltd
Wellwood, North Farm Road,
Tunbridge Wells, Kent, TN2 3DR, England

University of Notre Dame Press
Notre Dame, Indiana 46556, USA

First published in Great Britain and USA 1988

ISBN (UK) 0 85532 630 1

ISBN (USA) 0 268 01635 6
Library of Congress No: 88-50207

Typeset by Scribe Design, 123 Watling Street, Gillingham, Kent
Printed in Great Britain at the University Press, Cambridge

CONTENTS

Author's Introduction

In an earlier work (*Philosophy in Russia: From Herzen to Lenin and Berdyaev*, 1986) I devoted one chapter to the thought of Vladimir Solovyev and two chapters to the leading Russian religious philosophers who either emigrated after the events of 1917, as did Shestov, or were expelled from the Soviet Union in 1922, as was the case with most of them. There were, however, aspects and themes of Russian religious thought which were treated only briefly in the book and which I hoped to develop on another occasion. Hence the present work, which deals with selected aspects of Russian religious thought but makes no claim to cover the whole field. Apart from some references to Kireevsky and Khomyakov, I have confined my attention to Solovyev and his spiritual heirs of the first half of the twentieth century, and then only to certain lines of thought.

The western reader (and not only the western reader) of the writings of Russian religious philosophers can hardly fail to notice the presence of beliefs, ideas and themes which anyone accustomed to a distinction between philosophy on the one hand, and Christian theology on the other, would classify as pertaining to theology. This applies in an obvious manner to Solovyev, but it also applies to the works of his spiritual successors, even if to some more clearly than to others. The western reader may very well feel inclined to wonder what the thinkers in question are about, what they imagine that they are doing, and what their aims are. In the first two chapters, therefore, which are of an introductory nature, I have tried to put the relevant writers in their historical context and to explain how they were trying to meet what they regarded as a crying need. If anyone wishes to describe them as religious thinkers rather than as religious philosophers, well and good.

In philosophical thought in Russia the destiny or mission of the Russian nation has formed a common enough theme. The so-called problem of Russia, however, has been seen and treated within the framework of some general speculative theory of human history. And in the third chapter some of the ideas expounded by Russian religious thinkers in the field of philosophy of history are explained and discussed. The treatment is, of course, selective and relatively brief, but a good deal of what is said in the following chapter, on Godmanhood, is also relevant to this theme.

The subject of Godmanhood, discussed in the fourth chapter, obviously constitutes one of those topics which it is natural to regard as pertaining to Christian theology, especially as it is closely linked with the doctrine of the Incarnation. At the same time we have to remember that Solovyev's metaphysics was developed to a great extent precisely in his *Lectures on Godmanhood*, and that Berdyaev refers to Godmanhood as being one of the characteristic themes of creative religious philosophy in Russia. Further, Semyon Frank, who in important respects stood much closer to Solovyev than Berdyaev did, looked on the idea of Godmanhood as essential to any adequate philosophical anthropology. The fact of the matter is that, if one proposes to treat at all of Russian religiously oriented philosophers (or 'thinkers'), one has to take them as they come. If all the themes which some would consign to Christian theology were omitted, the area of discussion would be drastically reduced, and the interests of the relevant writers would be seriously misrepresented.

In the chapter on Solovyev in *Philosophy in Russia* I made some remarks about the theory of Sophia, or Wisdom. Although, it was Solovyev who effectively introduced Sophiology into religiously inspired philosophy in Russia, the theme was developed by two theologians, Pavel Florensky and Sergey Bulgakov, rather than by thinkers who are commonly classified as philosophers, such as Frank or Berdyaev. Even in the case of a professional theologian, however, such as Bulgakov, a good deal of what can only be described as speculative philosophy or metaphysics is involved. The theory of Sophia was offered as a way of clarifying the idea of creation and explaining the relationship between God and the world. In other words, the theory was certainly put forward as possessing philosophical significance, even though the idea of divine Wisdom was originally derived from Scriptural passages. For a time at any rate the theory of Sophia was prominent in Russian religious thought, and writers such as Florensky and Bulgakov regarded it as having importance for both theology and philosophy. Whether one agrees or disagrees is obviously another question.

In his endeavour to develop a wide-reaching Christian world-view, a general and coherent religiously inspired interpretation of reality, Vladimir Solovyev, Russia's first systematic philosopher, tried to show how faith and reason, religious belief and speculative philosophy, are capable of living in harmony and making their own complementary contributions to a unified understanding of the world and of human life and history. It was his conviction that a really adequate philosophy would harmonize with Christian belief, support it, and form part of a general religious vision of reality. While, however, this idea was shared by some later Russian thinkers, such as S.L. Frank and N.O. Lossky (in spite of the latter's reservations about some of Solovyev's theories), it was challenged by Leon Shestov (Lev Schwarzman) who saw speculative philosophy and religious faith as sharply opposed to one another. Whereas for Solovyev it was a case of Both/And, for Shestov it was definitely a case of Either/Or. In *Philosophy in Russia* I included a section on Shestov's attitude to philosophy on the one hand and religious faith on the other hand; but in the sixth chapter of this book the subject is treated at considerably greater length.

Solovyev died in 1900, and as well-known thinkers who are customarily described as being his spiritual heirs or successors are also dead, it is natural to ask whether the sort of religiously inspired thought which they represented was simply a passing phase in Russia's intellectual life or whether the movement has continued, if not in the Soviet Union itself then among Russians living abroad. One may also wonder, of course, whether the sort of themes which are discussed in this book could possibly be of interest to people today, especially perhaps if they have been educated in the Soviet Union and encouraged to regard all religiously inspired thought as outmoded. The point at issue is not, of course, whether there are still religious believers of various sorts in the Soviet Union and in Russian circles abroad, for there certainly are such believers, some of them being very well-known. The question is whether a movement of philosophical thought has continued, whether, that is to say, those who can reasonably be regarded as Solovyev's successors in the first half of the twentieth century have their successors in turn. If not, is it at all reasonable to suppose that such successors are likely to arise?

In the concluding chapter of this book I discuss topics of this kind, without claiming, however, to be able to provide adequate answers to the questions raised, and still less to possess any reliable prevision of the future. It is more a matter of not wanting to run away from and avoid discussing questions which are pretty well bound to occur to the reader's mind than of claiming to be in possession of inside information. I make no such claim.

As there are frequent references in the opening chapters of this book to the Russian intelligentsia, it is worthwhile my giving here some explanation of my use of the term. In the first place it must be understood that, to be a member of the Russian intelligentsia, is not the same thing as to be an 'intellectual'. A man or woman could qualify for being described as an intellectual even if he or she remained entirely aloof from social-political problems and interests, whereas the members of what is called the Russian intelligentsia were definitely committed from a social-political point of view and tended to subordinate all other interests to attainment of some social-political goal. In the middle decades of the nineteenth century in Russia there emerged a group of people who came mainly from families of Orthodox priests, doctors, merchants, petty officials (members, that is to say, of the nascent middle class, between the nobility on the one hand and the peasantry on the other), and who were united in their alienation from and hostility to the existing political regime. Opposed to the autocracy, they regarded themselves as the champions and spokesmen of an oppressed, ignorant and (apart from sudden furious peasant uprisings) inarticulate multitude. They did not all share the same ideas of what form of society should succeed the autocracy or how the change should be effected, but they were all convinced that the actual social-political structure should not be allowed to continue and deserved to perish. It was to this group of people that the term 'Russian intelligentsia' was first applied. The emergence of the intelligentsia in the sense indicated was made possible by growing facilities for education, and the further spread of education naturally tended to increase the ranks of the intelligentsia; but at all stages its members regarded themselves as the spearhead of radical social-political change and as called to enlighten and lead the generally dormant and voiceless masses. In the minds of the *intelligenty*, as the members of the intelligentsia came to be called, actions which promoted attainment of the desired social-political goal were thereby justified, whatever conservative moralists might say.

It is natural to think of the Russian intelligentsia as being devoted to the cause of revolution. Up to a point this idea is justified. For by the period with which we are concerned in the opening chapters of this book most of those who desired radical change had become increasingly sceptical of the likelihood of the regime itself initiating such change, or even of its agreeing to the desired changes except under pressure which it could not safely resist (as happened in 1905–6 at the close of the Russo-Japanese war). Any radical change therefore would have to be brought about by pressure 'from below'; and in this sense the intelligentsia in general can be said to have entertained the idea of revolution, in the sense, that is to say, that its members were convinced that the autocracy would be most unlikely to yield to anything but a degree of pressure from below which it could not in practice resist, and that the requisite pressure should accordingly be exerted. But it by no means follows that all the members of the intelligentsia hankered after violent or bloody revolution or after complete destruction of existing structures with a view to constructing something entirely new and without any organic connection with what went before. The anarchists, it is true, wanted the complete destruction of the state, but the official view of the Social Democrats (Marxists) was that the overthrow of the autocracy would have to be followed by a period of bourgeois democracy, until Russia was ripe for a take-over by the proletariat. (To be sure, Lenin was to jump the gun in 1917, but this fact does not make official Marxist doctrine other than it was.) The Socialist Revolutionaries, the successors of the Populists, were what their name implies, but one can hardly exclude from the ranks of the Russian intelligentsia the liberal thinkers who hoped for a non-violent transformation of the autocracy into a constitutional monarchy of the English type or its replacement by a democratic republic. In terms of the events of 1917 the first phase or stage of the revolution, namely the establishment of the Provisional Government, was more or less to their taste, but certainly not the subsequent Bolshevik seizure of power.

The Russian intelligentsia had, of course, other characteristics besides being committed to the cause of liberating the country from what was seen as the oppressive yoke of Tsarism. For example, the general outlook of the intelligentsia was positivist, materialist and opposed to the Church, if not to all religion. Obviously, many *intelligenty* were idealists in the sense that they had ideals which they hoped to realize, but idealism in this sense was not regarded as incompatible with philosophical positivism and materialism. In any case mention of positivism and materialism as component factors in the general outlook of the members of the intelligentsia does not provide any grounds for objecting to the main point which I have been trying to make, namely that the phrase 'the Russian intelligentsia' should not be understood as referring exclusively to those people who were convinced that liberation of the Russian people and establishment of a better society would be possible only through drastic, violent revolution, and who therefore desired and planned appropriate action. The phrase can be understood in a somewhat wider sense, and in the following pages I have often employed it in this way. When I refer specifically to the 'revolutionary' (or sometimes 'radical') intelligentsia, I have in mind the far Left, as distinct from those members of the intelligentsia who would describe themselves as 'liberals' of some sort and who hoped that the autocracy could be brought to an end without any violent cataclysm. Sometimes, of course, the context makes it sufficiently clear whether a reference to the Russian intelligentsia should be understood in the wider or the narrower sense.

I should perhaps add that I have not included a separate bibliography in this book. The principal sources I have used are mentioned in the text and footnotes; otherwise a relevant bibliography is given in my *Philosophy in Russia*, mentioned at the outset of this Introduction.

Chapter 1

Religious thought in Russia (1)

The idea of religious belief forming an unquestioned background to or framework for life certainly has its attractions. For then it is conceived as something which is always there and available, something on which one can fall back for reassurance, something on which one can rely, in a manner analogous to the way in which children in a united family know instinctively that they can rely on parental love. This sort of simple and unquestioning Christian faith was not infrequently attributed to the peasantry of pre-revolutionary Russia. To be sure, the eminent literary and social critic Vissarion Belinsky asserted, in his famous *Letter to N.V. Gogol*, that the Russian people was deeply atheistic by nature and that any religiosity which it manifested was only skin-deep. Genuine religious feeling, according to Belinsky, could be found only among the schismatics, the Old Believers, who were quite different from the great mass of the people. Doestoevsky, however, as his readers must be aware, while admitting that the Russian peasants were ignorant of even basic principles of Christian belief, none the less claimed that the love of Christ was deeply rooted in their hearts. The great novelist liked to maintain that religious truth was best preserved among the simple peasants, who were free from the sceptical questioning inspired by contact with or imitation of western Europe with its boasted enlightenment. The peasant's faith was unencumbered with theology and tended to be mixed up with a good deal of error and superstition; but it was the faith which constituted a shared background to life, shared, that is to say, by the members of the peasant community, as distinct from the intelligentsia and the more educated members of the gentry.

When it is a question of assessing the religious faith of the peasants in pre-revolutionary Russia, we are obviously not committed to choosing

1

between the more unqualified generalizations of Belinsky on the one hand, or Dostoevsky on the other. Commenting on Dostoevsky's view of the peasantry as the depository of Christian truth and of the educated classes as apostates from this truth, Konstantin Dmitrievich Kavelin, a scholar and a liberal in politics, remarked that he could not see the bulk of the peasantry as custodians of Christian truth and that, in his opinion, Dostoevsky's picture of them could not survive critical scrutiny. Still, even if one agrees with Kavelin that Dostoevsky was inclined to create for himself an unrealistic and too rosy a picture of the Russian peasant, one may still believe that in claiming, as he did, that in the Russian people there was not a trace of religious feeling Belinsky was guilty of exaggeration. Both Belinsky and Dostoevsky were inclined to see what they wanted to see. This was not so difficult when the peasant was looked at from a considerable distance. In any case the idea of simple unquestioning faith as a background to life may still have its attractions, irrespective of the question whether such faith was or was not exemplified in the nineteenth-century Russian peasantry.

Sooner or later, however, thought is bound to arise, thought that is to say which takes religion for its object. Such thought can, of course, assume a variety of forms. It can arise within the area of religious faith, exploring for example the relations between or the implications of beliefs which the thinker presupposes and claims to accept, or examining ways in which it might be shown that it is reasonable to accept such beliefs. In other words, thinking about the Christian religion can take the form of Christian theology or of apologetics. It is obvious, however, that when thought takes religion as its object for reflection, it may do so in a questioning, sceptical or even downright hostile spirit. It may be argued, for instance, that there is no good ground for claiming that this or that doctrine is true. Or attention may be focused more on what are alleged to be the deplorable social consequences of religious belief and practice.

Even if we are prepared to accept Dostoevsky's claim that in comparison with the educated classes of the country the peasants of Russia were the custodians of religious faith, it would obviously be both useless and absurd to look to the peasantry for any systematic theological or philosophical thought from within the area of faith. There is no need to labour this point. For the matter of that, the achievements of the official representatives of the Russian Orthodox Church in the fields of Christian theology and religiously inspired or oriented philosophy were hardly impressive. Among the parish clergy the level of education was, generally speaking, low. The priest had, of course, to be able to celebrate the liturgy and administer the sacraments, but in many respects his life resembled that of the peasants. The monks, from among whom the bishops were taken, had more opportunity for study and prayer; but they looked back to the writings of the Fathers, for example, and showed little enthusiasm for exploring fresh avenues of thought. There were indeed some learned professors in the theological academies, but their influence on the minds of educated Russians was not extensive. The Russian Orthodox Church was capable of producing examples of holiness such as St Seraphim of Sarov (1759–1833) and charismatic figures such as Father John of Kronstadt (1828–1908). Further, some highly educated people, as well as more ordinary folk, took to visiting certain monasteries with a view to consulting 'Elders' with a reputation for the gift of spiritual discernment. For a fictional portrait of such an Elder we have only to turn to Dostoevsky's Father Zosima as presented in *The Brothers Karamazov*. But though there were doubtless a good many people who found solace and strength in the liturgical life of the Church or in the counsel of monks with a reputation for holiness, the Church was certainly not held in high esteem from the intellectual point of view. Generally speaking, the educated class tended to despise the Church and expect little from it.

To place all the blame for this on the Church alone would be unfair. In the Middle Ages, during the period of Tartar domination, the Church contributed powerfully to sustaining morale and encouraging a sense of nationhood. Further, we should recognize the fact that in the ensuing period of the rise and consolidation of Muscovite rule Orthodox prelates could on occasion bring themselves to rebuke their secular rulers for their conduct. The best known example is that of the Metropolitan Philip who sternly admonished Ivan IV (the Terrible) for his cruel excesses and, for his pains, was thrown into prison and murdered. But from the time of Peter the Great, at any rate, the Russian Orthodox Church was reduced to the position of a department of state and made entirely subservient to the autocracy. The monarchs posed, of course, as patrons and protectors of the Church. And so they were in a sense. But they looked on the Church as a valuable instrument in maintaining faith in the Tsar and acceptance of his rule. Innovative thinking within the Church was not encouraged, to put it mildly. It was the Church's business to preserve intact the doctrines laid down by the Councils which were recognized as authoritative by the Orthodox world and to support the autocracy. It is hardly going too far if one says that the less genuine thought there was on the part of the clergy, the better pleased was the regime. Thought was regarded as potentially unsettling, and it was not the Church's job to unsettle minds.

The official Russian Orthodox Church was not, of course, the only religious body. There were, for example, the schismatics, the so-called Old Believers. We have to remember, however, that when the schism occurred in the seventeenth century, during the reign of Tsar Alexis, the schismatics did not break away from the parent body because they demanded changes which the official Church was unwilling to grant. On the contrary, it was a case of refusing to accept the small liturgical and ritual reforms imposed by the Patriarch Nikon in conjunction with the Tsar. The Old Believers certainly had their virtues. Their behaviour in the face of persecution was remarkable, and later they provided stalwart representatives of the merchant class. But original or independent thought in the religious sphere was not among their qualities. One would hardly expect it to be. As for the members of the various sects, they were by no means all fanatics or 'enthusiasts', but they tended to be simple people, not given to abstract thought. It should be added that the schismatics and sectarians were, in respect to religion, what might be described as second-class citizens, in the sense that they were subject to various degrees of repression or restriction. It was not until 1905, in the course of the first revolution, that religious bodies outside the official Orthodox Church were granted full freedom and autonomous status.

This move left the Russian Orthodox Church in the unenviable position of being the one religious body which lacked any real degree of autonomy. Proposals were made to remedy the situation, but Konstantin Pobedonostsev (1827–1907), Over-Procurator of the Holy Synod, who was opposed to change on principle, succeeded in preventing their implementation. On his death further plans were made, but although the Tsar (Nicholas II) seemed favourably disposed towards them, he procrastinated so long that the revolution of March 1917 (February Old Style) occurred before anything had been done.

While the official Russian Orthodox Church was becoming more and more identified with the interests of the regime, western thought was gradually obtaining a hold on the minds of those educated Russians who were open to fresh and unsettling ideas. During the reign of Catherine the Great (1762–96), at any rate up to the time of the French revolution and the execution of Louis XVI, the ideas of the French Enlightenment penetrated Russia with the empress's approval. Until events in France suggested that flirting with the ideas of *les philosophes* could be dangerous, she liked to think of herself as a disciple of Voltaire. Obviously, 'Russian Voltaireanism', as the thought of the Enlightenment as transmitted to Russia has been called, was not likely to strenghten simple and unquestioning religious belief. This could be left to the clergy and peasants, while those members of the gentry who were affected by the ideas from western Europe adopted a more sceptical attitude.'

As one might expect, the influence in Russia of the thought of the Enlightenment was succeeded, in the first half of the nineteenth century, by that of German idealism. For a while the ideas of Schelling and Hegel were much discussed by students and hastily applied to Russian problems. In the middle decades of the century, however, positivist, materialist and utilitarian lines of thought supplanted the influence of German idealism, especially among members of the emerging radical intelligentsia, young people who, for the most part, came neither from the ranks of the nobility, nor from the peasantry, but rather from a middle level of the population, being children of priests, doctors, or petty officials. This radical intelligentsia was, of course, alientated from the regime, and this meant that it was alienated also from the Church, as a firm supporter of the *status quo*. Its members regarded the doctrines of the Church as so much falsehood and superstition, as incompatible with a scientific outlook and as obstacles in the way of progress and education; but their hostility towards the Church was motivated much more by their conviction that the Church was simply a lackey of a hated political regime and a hindrance to the creation of a more rational and just social order, a society of free and mature human beings. In their view the Church was guilty not only of omission, of doing nothing to further urgently needed social-political reform, but also of commission, of encouraging the regime to resist demands for change.

The ideas of those writers, such as Nikolai Chernyshevsky (1828–89), Nikolai Dobrolyubov (1836–61) and Dmitry Pisarev (1840–68), who influenced or even inspired the young members of the Russian radical intelligentsia in the 1850s and 1860s may not have been profound, but they embodied a world-view which became widespread among those educated Russians who looked on themselves as enlightened, up-to-date and concerned with promoting the common good through the reform of society. Theology and metaphysics were regarded as outmoded and best forgotten; science was conceived both as the one reliable path to knowledge and as an indispensable means for the improvement of society, and for promoting the welfare and happiness of mankind. Further, social utility was looked upon as the criterion for deciding moral issues and even for judging the value of literature and art. The autocracy, needless to say, was judged to be not only useless but harmful; and a similar verdict was passed on the Russian Orthodox Church. At the time, of course, the limits of what could be openly said or written were pretty narrow. In 1862 Chernyshevsky was arrested and, after trial, sent to Siberia, a fate which made him a martyr and hero to the intelligentsia. Pisarev was arrested and imprisoned in 1862, on the ground of incitement to revolution. But in the minds of the intelligentsia such events simply served to strengthen the general outlook inspired or communicated by the writers in question.

The official Russian Orthodox Church had little to offer by way of an intellectually impressive and persuasive alternative to the world-outlook which was coming to prevail in the student world. It could, of course, repeat its traditional doctrines, and it could support measures taken by the state to exercise censorship over what was publicly said or written. But the clergy at any rate seemed unable to speak to the alienated in a way which was likely to make any real impression on their minds, for example by showing the relevance of a religious world-view to issues which were considered important by the members of the intelligentsia themselves. There were, of course, a number of genuinely learned clergy, in the theological academies in particular. For the matter of that, Chernyshevsky's father was a highly educated priest in the city of Saratov. But the character of their training made it difficult for the clergy to communicate with the sort of young people who formed the radical intelligentsia. Besides, as we have seen, awareness of the social injustices perpetrated or countenanced by the political regime was apt to be accompanied by a hostile or even contemptuous attitude to the Church as a lackey of the autocracy. That this association between the regime and the official Russian Orthodox Church was not devoid of foundation in fact obviously did not make things any easier for the clergy if they wished to influence the minds of the intelligentsia. What they said was apt to be regarded as coming from a tainted source.

The shortcomings of the Russian Orthodox clergy have doubtless at times been exaggerated. According to Belinsky, for example, the Church was nothing but a toady and a determined enemy of equality and of human brotherhood, while the Russian priests were everywhere regarded (and justly, Belinsky implies) as symbols of gluttony, drunkenness, avarice, sycophancy and bawdiness. All that Belinsky can say in favour of the Russian priest is that it is more appropriate to accuse him of indifference in matters of faith than of fanaticism or intolerance. The trouble with such generalizations, however, is that the genuine goodness of at least some priests and monks is passed over, left unmentioned. There were always some who kept alive the tradition of deep spirituality, of interiority, of prayer and charity, within Orthodoxy. If, however, we leave out of account the *yurodivye* ('holy fools' is the traditional English phrase) who from time to time performed the useful function of rebuking tyrants to their faces, deep spirituality tended to be mentally associated with the thought of certain monasteries and of hermits living deep in the forests among the wild animals. In other words, the holy man was conceived as someone who had retreated from the world and to whom people might go for aid and counsel rather than as striding outwards to people with a message which was relevant to their problems within the world. While the members of the intelligentsia did not conceive western Europe as heaven on earth, they none the less looked on 'Holy Russia', in so far as it ever existed at all, as belonging to the past.

From the Christian point of view, the need was not so much for criticism of the ideas of the intelligentsia, criticism which was likely to be based on premises not accepted by its members, as for presentation of an alternative world-outlook, a religiously oriented one, one which was capable of arresting the attention of those who were alienated from religion and the relevance of which to the urgent problems of Russia could be shown. In so far as we can justifiably talk about *a* radical ideology (thus tending to imply the existence of one uniform and coherent whole), this ideology clearly filled a spiritual void, inasmuch as it was geared to freeing Russia from evils which were only too obviously real and prevalent and did not recommend putting up with these evils or simply cultivating the virtue of patience. It could be effectively countered only by another positive world-view, one which also held out a promise of transforming society for the better but which at the same time did justice to aspects of reality and of the human being and human life to which the members of the intelligentsia were blind.

In the first half of the nineteenth century this need was seen by several Russian laymen, while a sustained attempt to meet it was later made by another layman, Vladimir Solovyev. In the next section some general remarks will be made about the line of thought which they represented, and about the reception accorded it at the time.

II

A call for a philosophy issuing from Christian faith and remaining in harmony with it was voiced by Slavophile writers such as Ivan Kireevsky (1806–56) and Aleksey Khomyakov (1804–60). These writers are probably best known to western students of Russian history for their negative attitude to Peter the Great's 'opening to the West', and for their tendency (manifested much more by Kireevsky than by Khomyakov) to idealize pre-Petrine Russia. But their call for a philosophy which would remain within, so to speak, the area of Christian faith was closely related to their assessment of the history, spirit and culture of western Europe.

They saw western thought as having become increasingly imbued with rationalism, with belief in the omnicompetence of reason when it was a question of coming to know truth. In medieval Christendom the domination of rationalism had been held in check up to a point, but in spite of protests from this or that thinker (Pascal, for example) it was rationalism which won the victory, and philosophy became either detached from or hostile to religion. Though Peter the Great was interested in making use of western technology and military skill, but not in philosophy, his opening to the West none the less facilitated the spread of western rationalism in Russia. To be sure, apart from Patristic thought and its derivatives, Russia had little of her own which was capable of counterbalancing western philosophical thought, and the importation of western ideas therefore was understandable. But this does not alter the fact that these ideas were to a large extent alien to the traditions of the Holy Russia to which the Slavophile thinkers tended to look back with nostalgia. As a literal return to the past was out of the question, there was an urgent need for Russia to develop her own philosophy in close union with her religious tradition. Western philosophical thought had revealed itself as inimical to religious faith, and, as imported into Russia, it had manifested the same characteristic. To remedy this state of affairs philosophical thought in Russia should be developed on the basis of religious faith rather than outside the sphere of faith or as hostile to it. In other words, what was needed was renewal of the approach shared by the Greek Fathers of the Church, such as St Gregory of Nyssa, who had philosophized as Christian believers and not as people who claimed to represent or embody pure Reason. If Russia were to succeed in lifting up reason into union with religious faith, she would provide a guiding light for other nations too.

It would be a mistake to suppose that because a thinker such as Kireevsky desired the development of a philosophy animated by the spirit of the Greek Fathers of the Church, he was simply an antiquarian, in the sense that he demanded a return to a far distant past. In Kireevsky's view, anyone wishing to contribute to the development in question could profitably reflect on the later philosophizing of the German idealist Schelling, not as a set of doctrines to be accepted but as a point of departure for personal thought, as an example, that is to say, of religiously oriented philosophy. What Kireevsky really had in mind was, of course, the creation of a general Christian world-view, not simply as a mental exercise but as a background to or framework for life.

A passing reference has been made to Pascal. One line of thought on which Kireevsky laid emphasis was the need for integrating the powers of the soul and for their cooperation in the search for truth. In western thought as he saw it, there had been an hypertrophy of the analytic and deductive reason; and he strongly sympathized with Pascal's famous statement that the heart has its reasons which Reason cannot understand. It can hardly be asserted that Kireevsky made his idea of the desired recovery of 'mental wholeness' crystal clear; but his opposition to rationalism is clear enough. Reason, he argued, cannot possibly be the only means of attaining true knowledge. We cannot, for example, get along without sense-experience, as the empiricists have shown. And Kireevsky envisaged both religious and aesthetic experience as contributing to the attainment of truth.

The shortcomings of rationalism were also emphasized by Khomyakov. Reason obviously has its part to play in the attainment of truth. Discernment of the logical relations between concepts and propositions is the work of reason. But we cannot gain knowledge of external reality simply by noting such relations. Immediate knowledge of given, existing reality is required, an immediate knowledge or intuitive apprehension which Khomyakov called 'faith'. But by faith in this context he meant simply an intuitive grasp of an object, say a tree, as existing. Faith or immediate knowledge in this sense was regarded by Khomyakov as preceding the logical use of reason and as something which is experienced by every human being. Faith in a religious sense is not common to all human beings but is attributable to them only in so far as they are genuine members of a religious community united by mutual love. None the less, faith in this second sense also has a role to play in the discernment of truth, and Khomyakov called for the integration, or reintegration, of faith and reason. Both Kireevsky and Khomyakov were careful not to attack reason as such. Both conceived rationalism as a disease of reason (the hypertrophy of reason), a disease which could be cured. Both men hoped that Russian thinkers would be able to effect the cure.

Kireevsky desired, in effect, the creation of a developed Christian world-view, an up-to-date version, so the speak, of the simpler world-view presented in patristic literature. But although he indicated some of the lines of thought which, in his opinion, should be followed up, he did not himself provide the projected synthesis. Nor did Khomyakov. In the second half of the nineteenth century, however, Vladimir Solovyev

(1853–1900), Russia's first really systematic philosopher, tried to show how faith and reason, religious belief and speculative philosophy, are capable of living in harmony and making their own contributions to a unified understanding of the world and of human life and history.

On the one hand Solovyev was faced by thought which was at best indifferent and often positively hostile to religion in general and Christianity in particular, or at any rate to the Church. On the other hand he saw a Church which was profoundly suspicious of all new ideas and which had signally failed to produce any living thought to which educated Russians, let alone the alienated youth, would be likely to give serious consideration. In his opinion, however, the oppositions which, from an historical point of view, had tended to grow between philosophy and Christian faith, science and religion, were by no means inevitable or something which one could only accept and endure. He insisted therefore on the need for thought which would be inspired by or issue from Christian faith and which would interpret the world and human life and history in the light of the faith but in a manner which would mean something to minds constantly exposed to claims that religion and science are irreconcilably opposed, that there are no absolute values, and that metaphysical speculation is simply a waste of time and of no benefit to society. It was Solovyev's conviction that the alleged opposition between philosophy and religious faith was due, to a great extent, to inadequate, one-sided and distorting ideas of philosophy. A really adequate philosophy would harmonize with Christian belief, support it and form part of a comprehensive, religiously oriented world outlook. Solovyev hoped to succeed in constructing a kind of map which would exhibit the places and relations between philosophy, religious faith, scientific inquiry of various kinds, and moral and aesthetic experience in a unified interpretation of reality.

As a boy of fourteen Solovyev embraced atheism, materialism and socialism. But at the age of sixteen his reading of Spinoza, succeeded by study of German philosophers (Kant and his successors), turned his mind back towards religion, and by the time he was eighteen he had regained his Christian faith. His interpretation of his religious belief, however, was not unaffected by his early philosophical studies. For his reading of Spinoza and of the German idealists implanted, or at any rate contributed powerfully to strengthening, the idea of 'total-unity', of the Absolute, of reality as a coherent and intelligible whole, which became a conspicuous feature of his thought. Given the guiding idea of total-unity, Solovyev was naturally stimulated to endeavour to overcome such apparent or alleged oppositions as those between science and religion, philosophy and religious faith. As we shall presently see, he spoke of philosophy in different ways at different times; but in a dissertation, presented in the University of Moscow and published in 1874, he referred to the need for a restoration of the inner unity of the intellectual world and, in particular, for a synthesis of science, philosophy and religion[1]. The instrument for achieving any such synthesis would, of course, be philosophical reflection; but Solovyev saw no good reason why philosophy should not reflect on itself, as well as on science and religion.

Solovyev made an impressive contribution to philosophical literature. Thus in 1877 he published his work on *The Philosophical Foundations of Intergral Knowledge*, and in the following year his *Lectures on Godmanhood*, in which he expounded his religious metaphysics. He also wrote on matters pertaining to political theory and to philosophy of history, the first volume of his *History and Future of Theocracy* appearing in 1884 and his *Three Conversations on War, Progress and the End of Universal History* in 1889. His ethical work, *The Justification of the Good*, appeared in 1897 (second edition, 1898), and at the close of his life he was working on his *Foundations of Theoretical Philosophy*, which remained unfinished at this death.

Solovyev was also a poet, and for a period he interested himself actively in what we now call ecumenism. In 1889 he published in French his *Russia and the Universal Church (La Russie et l'église universelle)*.

Although Solovyev was Russia's first systematic philosopher and a thinker of considerable stature, his thought received little attention from those whom he was particularly concerned with influencing. To be sure, his public lectures on Godmanhood attracted a distinguished audience. Both Dostoevsky and Tolstoy figured among his hearers. But, as Berdyaev was later to say, 'the Russian intelligentsia did not read him

---

1. *Sobranie sochinenii* (Collected Works), 10 vols., Brussels, 1966, vol. I, p. 151. This photographic edition of the 1911–14 St Petersburg edition will be referred to as *SS*. The quotation is from *The Crisis of Western Philosophy*, 5.

and did not know him. And it did not regard him as one of its own.'[2] This neglect is not, indeed, altogether surprising. If one reads Solovyev's *Lectures on Godmanhood* one would hardly expect the members of the radical intelligentsia to show much enthusiasm for such abstruse metaphysics, far removed from their own predominantly positivist and materialist ways of thinking. If they were aware of what Solovyev was saying, they would look on him as giving news from nowhere and as developing lines of thought which had no relevance to what they judged to be the important issues in contemporary Russian life. But in the early years of the twentieth century the climate of thought in Russia changed, and it became easier for religiously oriented thought to receive a hearing. More will be said in Chapter 3 about this development, but to suggest that Solovyev was a failure or that he had no influence would be wrong. For he had his spiritual heirs and successors. In his lifetime, however, the radical intelligentsia did not pay him much attention.

III

At this point it is as well to pause and ask how Solovyev conceived his function as a philosopher. As noted, he desired the development of a philosophy which would in some sense issue from faith and remain within the area of faith. How should this idea be understood? Did Solovyev conceive the kind of philosophy he had in mind as assuming the truth of Christian doctrines and as using these truths as premises for further reasoning? If so, would it not be more appropriate to speak of Christian theology than of philosophy? In one work he ascribes to philosophy the task of justifying the faith of 'our fathers', and this may suggest the idea of Christian apologetics. But when he goes on to explain that, by justifying the faith of our fathers he means 'raising it to a new stage of rational consciousness'[3], is it not reasonable to conclude that he has in mind an activity which, in the West, is generally described

---

2. *Landmarks. A Collection of Essays on the Russian Intelligentsia*, 1909, edited by Boris Shragin and Albert Todd, translated by Marion Schwartz, p. 17 (New York, 1977). This translation will be referred to in notes as *L*. An English translation is also printed in *Canadian Slavic Studies* (1968–71); but for the convenience of readers references have been made to *L*, even when the wording of quotations differs from that in *L*.

3. *SS*, IV, p. 243. From *The History and Future of Theocracy*.

as Christian theology? Or should we conclude that he has in mind, in effect, the transformation of theology into philosophy? After all, in his *Lectures on Godmanhood*, he gives what might be described as a philosophical version of the doctrine of the Trinity or as a transformation of faith into metaphysics. Should we understand the task of justifying the faith of 'our fathers' by raising it to a new level of rational consciousness as being equivalent to the substitution of knowledge for faith, the rationalization, so to speak, of faith?

It is worth remarking that in later years, when writing his *Foundations of Theoretical Philosophy*, Solovyev asserted that the only thing which the convinced adherent of a positive religion is really entitled to hope for is that the philosopher 'by the free investigation of truth'[4] should attain agreement between his philosophical convictions and the dogmas of his religion—'a result which would be equally satisfactory for both sides'[5]. There is nothing here about using Christian doctrines as premises in philosophical reasoning, and it may appear that Solovyev has radically changed his mind. But though he has certainly come to insist more on the autonomy of philosophy and on the philosopher's duty to leave no presuppositions unexamined, we should bear in mind that, when Solovyev said or implied that genuine philosophy should presuppose faith, we are not entitled to take it for granted that he was referring to 'truths of faith', in the sense of Christian dogmas. What he had in mind was often not so much a set of doctrines as religious experience, in the sense of an intuitive apprehension of ultimate reality. In his view an adequate philosophy, one, that is to say, which is not narrowly one-sided or distorted, must be based not only on sense-experience, nor only on preception of the logical relations between abstract concepts, but also on an intellectual intuition of reality. Whether or not we are prepared to recognize the possibility of an intuitive apprehension of metaphenomenal reality, it is clear that to demand that the philosopher should allow for intuition as a source of knowledge is not at all the same thing as asserting that the philosopher should assume the truth of Christian doctrines, or that he should try to demonstrate their truth by transforming them into conclusions of

4. *SS*, IX, p. 95. From *Theoretical Philosophy*, I, 4.

5. *Ibid.*

philosophical reasoning. Obviously the fact that, by presupposing faith, Solovyev is sometimes referring to recognition of intellectual intuition of the ultimate reality as a source of knowledge does not warrant the conclusion that the relevant statements must always be interpreted in this sense. But at any rate it shows that it is a mistake to jump to the conclusion that Solovyev is simply pursuing theological reflection while describing it as philosophy.

Solovyev spoke in rather different ways, on different occasions, about the nature and functions of philosophy, and it is really a waste of time to persist in trying to find one uniform definition or concept, especially as there is no great difficulty in discerning some of his main guiding ideas. For example, he certainly believed that Christianity was presented by the official Church in a thoroughly inadequate form, that this fact was largely responsible for the alienation from religion of so many educated people and of the student youth, and that there was a crying need for the faith to be raised, as he put it, to a new level of religious consciousness. But a more adequate theological presentation of Christianity, in a narrow sense of theology, would not be enough. Religion, Solovyev argued[6], had been gradually pushed to the periphery of life (when it was accorded a place at all), whereas it should be all or nothing. That is to say, genuine religion should premeate the whole of human life, inspiring all human activities. There was thus a real need to develop a broad Christian world-view, a religiously oriented interpretation of the world and of human life and history, a world-view which could be a guide to life. Solovyev spoke sometimes of religion and sometimes of philosophy as having a directive or guiding function in life. But it would clearly be a mistake to interpret him as meaning that the human being needed to be guided in life by philosophy as it is now understood in the departments of philosophy in most universities of the English-speaking world. He obviously had in mind philosophy in the sense of a general Christian interpretation of the world and human life. Philosophy in this sense pursued theoretical truth, but it also had a practical function. In accordance with his conviction that this is the case Solovyev wrote his large volume on ethics, *The Justification of the Good*. In it he made clear his belief that Christian wisdom or

6. *SS*, III, pp. 3–4. From *Lectures on Godmanhood*, I.

philosophy, in the sense of a general Christian interpretation of the
world and of human life and history, should govern not only the human
being's personal life and activity but also social, political and economic
life. For Solovyev, there was no sphere of human life and activity which
was exempt from the demands of morality. Unfortunately the Russian
Orthodox Church had failed to pay sufficient attention to this important truth.

In 1891 Solovyev read a paper at Moscow in which he maintained
that the Church had failed lamentably in promoting the realization of
the kingdom of God and that concern with social justice was being
shown by unbelievers rather than by believers. The former were acting
unconsciously as instruments of the divine Spirit. In view of this
attitude, and of Solovyev's insistence that moral values were relevant
not only to private life and relationships but to social-political life as
well, it may seem odd that the Russian radical intelligentsia in the
second half of the nineteenth century paid him so little attention.
Solovyev was indeed not 'one of their own'. He was a determined foe of
the positivist and materialist outlook which was so widespread among
the intelligentsia. Besides, the members of the intelligentsia were
inclined to write off without more ado not only religious believers,
including sincere ones, but also all appeals to absolute values or to an
absolute moral law. Further, Solovyev had been strongly influenced by
German idealism, and the radical intelligentsia, intent on the transformation of society and the attainment of socialism, had no use for
metaphysical speculation.

In the next chapter we shall have occasion to refer to the judgements
about the revolutionary intelligentsia which were expressed by some of
Solovyev's spiritual heirs.

Chapter 2

Religious thought in Russia (2)

The end of the nineteenth century witnessed a revival of art and poetry in Russian cultural life, a revival associated with such names as those of the poets and writers Vyacheslav Ivanov (1866–1949), Konstantin Balmont (1867–1943), Andrey Bely (Boris Bugaev, 1880–1934), and Alexander Blok (1880–1921), best known of the Russian Symbolists.

This renaissance in the literary and artistic spheres, sometimes described as Russia's 'Silver Age'[1], was accompanied in the area of philosophy by a reaction against the prevailing positivism and materialism. The reaction in question did not by any means always involve a return to the bosom of the Orthodox Church. There were various groups which were interested in religious problems, while standing aloof from institutional religion, and it is doubtless true that, as Christopher Read has suggested, all opponents of positivism and materialism tended to be regarded as 'religious'[2]. However this may be, the anti-positivist and anti-materialist reaction certainly created an atmosphere which was much more favourable to the sympathetic discussion of problems relating to religion and religious thought. A number of circles were formed which were frequented both by religious believers and by people who, while religiously uncommitted, were none the less interested in what one might describe as problems of life and

1. In distinction from the age of Pushkin and Lermontov, known as the Golden Age. Naturally enough, writers assign different approximate dates for the beginnings and ends of these 'ages'. Much depends on whether a writer is referring principally to poetry or to prose.

2. *Religion, Revolution and the Russian Intelligentsia, 1900–1912. The Vekhi Debate and Its Intellectual Background*, by Christopher Read, p. 38 (London, 1979).

17

who were prepared to discuss them with representatives of religious belief and others. Thus in 1901 a series of religious-philosophical meetings or assemblies was started at St Petersburg. Though, however, the Procurator of the Holy Synod had originally consented to the institution of this opportunity for dialogue, in 1903 he asked that an end be put to the meetings. He had become alarmed by the outspokenness of some of the participants.

In the same year, 1903, a collection of essays by different authors was published at Moscow with the title *Problems of Idealism (Problemy Idealizma)*, the editor being Pavel Novgorodtsev (1866–1924). Contributors to the volume included Nikolai Berdyaev (1874–1948), Semyon Frank (1877–1950), Sergey Bulgakov (1871–1944), and Bogdan Kistyakovsky (1868–1926). Several of these writers, such as Bulgakov, Frank and Berdyaev, had worked their way out of Marxism[3], finding themselves unable to accept the Marxist attitude to morality and values, as well, of course, as Marxism's materialist assumptions. As, however, the critique of positivism and materialism in *Problems of Idealism* was conducted on an academic level, with few fireworks, the volume did not arouse violent opposition or furious denunciation, even if it was regarded by the intelligentsia as a somewhat eccentric and potentially harmful production.

A far greater stir was caused by the publication in 1909 of the symposium *Vekhi (Landmarks*, though the title has sometimes been rendered as *Signposts)*. Contributors included some of those who had already written essays for *Problems of Idealism*, namely Berdyaev, Bulgakov, Frank and Kistyakovsky. These were joined by three newcomers, Mikhail Gerschenzon (1869–1925), Peter Struve (1870–1944) and Aleksandr Izgoev (A.S. Lande, 1872–1935).

The preface or foreword to *Vekhi* was written by Gerschenzon, a literary critic who edited the works of Chaadaev and Kireevsky and who insisted that the inner spiritual life of the individual human being is the only sure foundation for a desirable social structure. Struve had

---

3. These thinkers had been what is known as 'Legal Marxists' in the sense that they embraced Marxist theory, or some of it, but did not pursue underground revolutionary activity. One could expound and support Marxist economic theory, for example, under one's own name without necessarily incurring the wrath of the authorities.

been a Legal Marxist. Indeed, he had written a manifesto for the
convention of the Russian Social Democrats at Minsk in 1898. But even
while calling himself a Marxist, he had advocated cooperation with the
liberals with a view to securing political reforms and had therefore been
criticized by the revolutionary Marxists who disdained what they
regarded as shameful compromise. Abandoning Marxism, Struve became a devout Christian, a prominent liberal politician, and a champion of personal liberty and rights in the face of threats from either the
Right or the Left. As for Izgoev, the least known of the contributors to
Vekhi, he was a gifted publicist, who shared the belief in moral values
which was common to his fellow authors. Like Gerschenzon and Frank
he came of a Jewish family, but in the course of time he abandoned
religious belief. (Frank joined the Russian Orthodox Church in 1912.)

The main reason why *Vekhi* created a stir and aroused strong and
sometimes abusive protests was that it expressed outspoken criticism of
the Russian intelligentsia, criticism which was all the more telling as it
came from writers who had themselves been members of the radical
intelligentsia and knew its spirit from inside. As one might expect, the
intelligenty reacted by representing their critics as reactionaries. But it
would be a great mistake to assume that the contributors to *Vekhi* were
intent on supporting the autocracy. They were perfectly well aware of
the need for change, but they were convinced that society could not be
transformed for the better simply by the means advocated by members
of the intelligentsia. The revolutionaries, caught in the grip of what has
been described as the mystique of revolution, believed that if the
existing regime were completely overthrown, if a complete sweep could
be achieved, the establishment of a new social-political order—whether
by means of the dictatorship of the proletariat, as envisaged by the
revolutionary Marxists, or through the realization of 'Russian socialism', as desired by the Socialist Revolutionaries (the successors of the
Populists)— would automatically produce a better society, something
approaching a paradise on earth. That is to say, the revolutionaries
assumed that human beings are determined by their social environment,
that consciousness reflects the influence of social-political structures,
and that change in these structures causes a change in human consciousness. Do away with the oppressive regime by revolutionary
action, and human consciousness will be changed for the better. Even

among liberals, who desired gradual and progressive reform, not sudden and probably violent revolution, there were those who thought in a basically similar manner, namely that measures of political, economic and legal reform would be sufficient to produce better people and a better society.

The authors of *Vekhi*, however, were convinced that a moral and spiritual rebirth was required. Their criticism was directed primarily against the radical intelligentsia, against those who were caught in the grip of the revolutionary dream and who seemed to think that paradise on earth could be secured by promoting and intensifying class hatred, as though an increase in hatred were a sure means of bringing about an increase in love. But after the publication of *Vekhi* the volume was also attacked by liberals, who felt, quite justifiably, that they too were affected by the writers' line of criticism, in so far, that is to say, as they (liberal theorists) accepted, explicitly or implicitly, the view that it is social-political or economic structures which determine consciousness. The contributors to *Vekhi*, though some more obviously than others, insisted on the priority of moral values and on the freedom of the human person as such. Without an inner conversion, so to speak, changes in political, social and economic structures, whether sudden and sweeping or more gradual, would be unable to realize the higher type of society desired by the spokesmen of the intelligentsia. The authors of *Vehki* hoped that it might prove possible to open the eyes of members of the intelligentsia to the error of their ways before it was too late. Hindsight, of course, enables us to see that it was already too late.

In his contribution to *Vekhi* Berdyaev drew attention to the scant respect shown by the radical intelligentsia for objective truth. 'To this day our educated youth cannot admit the autonomous value of science, philosophy, education and universities'[4]. True, the revolutionary youth was ready enough to dismiss religion in the name of science; but its utilitarian way of thought did not allow it to ascribe to science anything more than a pragmatic value. Science, education and philosophy were regarded as valuable only to the extent in which they could be seen as instruments for attaining practical ends determined by the intelligentsia itself. 'The intelligentsia is prepared to accept on faith any philosophy

4. *L*, p. 6

that sanctions its social ideals ...'[5] Berdyaev recognized that an interest in theoretical truth simply for its own sake had never been strong in Russia, and that 'a feeble awareness of the unconditional value of truth'[6] was by no means confined to revolutionary youth. But, in his view, this deficiency was most clearly manifested among the members of the intelligentsia, for whom the attainment of this or that social-political goal was the paramount consideration. The defect in question showed itself, for example, in the intelligentsia's understanding of Marxism. That is to say, the objective aspect of Marxism, its economic analysis, was subordinated to emphasis on subjective elements such as class consciousness.

Semyon Frank, in his essay, argued that the members of the intelligentsia always subordinated theoretical, aesthetic and religious values to moral values, but that they then went on to throw overboard the idea of objective values in general. This, however, did not prevent them from stating their own social ideals in a thoroughly dogmatic manner. According to Frank, the 'classic Russian *intelligent*' could well be defined as a 'militant monk of the nihilistic religion of earthly well-being'[7]. Such a man had his own faith, and he was prepared to sacrifice himself for it; but he 'does not love living people, only his *idea*, the idea of universal human happiness'.[8] Frank was doubtless justified in representing the revolutionary intelligentsia as loving an abstraction, humanity in the abstract, rather than actual living men and women. This is apt to be true of all those who favour violent revolutionary action in the name of the future of mankind.

Writing on a more down-to-earth theme, namely 'in defence of law', Kistyakovsky asserted that 'the Russian intelligentsia never respected law nor saw any value in it'.[9] He was not, of course, blind to the fact that disrespect for the law was nothing new in Russia. In the nineteenth century Alexander Herzen had noted that the Russian, whatever his

5. *L*, p. 8

6. *L*, p. 9

7. *L*, p. 179

8. *L*, p. 170

9. *L*, p. 113

social class might be, was accustomed to break the law whenever he thought that it was safe to do so. Further, the government was given to behaving in the same sort of way. Kistyakovsky also conceded that the Slavophiles had encouraged disrespect for the law by claiming that a concern with 'formal justice' was the expression of a deplorable western mentality, to which Russians, with their alleged innate sense of a higher form of justice, rose superior. In other words, the members of the contemporary intelligentsia were heirs to a common enough Russian attitude to law. At the same time this attitude was obviously reinforced by the Marxist idea of law as an instrument of the dominant class. In Kistyakovsky's opinion, there was a serious need in Russia for a sound legal system, respected not only by private citizens but also by the government and bureaucracy. The members of the radical intelligentsia were doing no good service to the country by encouraging contempt for the law. The fact of the matter was that they lacked any real understanding of human rights and failed to see the need for a legal system to protect these rights.

Izgoev, in his essay, wrote about the breakdown of parental influence in the family life of the intelligentsia and about the morals (or lack of them) of university youth. But he tried to be fair. If the government mistrusted the student body, as was the case, it was itself very largely responsible for creating the grounds of this mistrust, for by its repressive policy and restrictive practices the regime had pushed the student youth more and more to the extreme Left, thus contributing to its alienation from the state. The result was that, when the Duma, the Russian parliament, was established after the 1905 revolution, many of the elected deputies were obstinately uncooperative and obstructive.

The idea of cooperation with the state was also treated by Peter Struve. He was aware that cooperation required goodwill on both sides, but he ventured the tentative prophecy that the intelligentsia would become progressively reconciled with the state, the rapidity of the process depending on the pace of Russia's economic development and of the reorganization of the political structure 'in a constitutional spirit'.[10] In other words, if the regime were to see the need of and actually to undertake serious political reform, there was a good chance

10. *L*, p. 197

of members of the intelligentsia progressively abandoning their un-cooperative attitude and their insistence that nothing short of revolu-tion would do any good and start working together with others for the good of the country. Struve's prophecy might perhaps have been fulfilled if the regime had avoided involvement in the 1914–18 war and had allowed the modest beginnings of constitutional reform to develop further at a reasonably rapid pace. But, as we know, things did not work out in this way.

Of all the contributors to *Vekhi* it was Gerschenzon who made the most biting remarks about the Russian intelligentsia. 'A crowd of sick men quarantined in their own country—that is the Russian intelligent-sia'.[11] Again, 'in Russia an almost infallible gauge of the strength of an artist's genius is the extent of his hatred for the intelligentsia. We need mention only the greatest of them: Tolstoy and Dostoevsky, Tyutchev and Fet'.[12] It is arguable, however, that Gerschenzon allowed his own dislike of the intelligentsia to lead him into some exaggeration. For example, while L.Tolstoy was far from being a member of what is ordinarily counted as the Russian intelligentsia, he had his reservations about *Vekhi* when it appeared, claiming to find a high degree of dogmatism and arrogance in the contents. As coming from Tolstoy, this line of criticism may sound a bit odd. But if one reads certain *Vekhi* essays, notably Gerschenzon's, one can hardly fail to see what the great man had in mind. Still, Gerschenzon would doubtless have heartily approved of Anton Chekhov's description of the intelligentsia in one of his letters as 'hypocritical, insincere, hysterical, uncultivated and lethar-gic',[13] even though Chekhov added that the oppressors of the intel-ligentsia had emerged from the same womb.

However, if Gerschenzon tended to take a uniformly dim view of the Russian intelligentsia, other contributors to *Vekhi* were prepared to recognize some good qualities in the *intelligenty*. For example, Ber-dyaev acknowledged their real concern with social justice, while Frank paid tribute to the revolutionary youth's readiness to sacrifice itself for

11. *L*, p. 79

12. *L*, p. 76

13. *Letters of Anton Chekhov*, selected and edited by Avrahm Yarmolinsky, p. 336 (London, 1974). From a letter of 22 February 1899, to Ivan Ivanovich Orlov.

its faith. Again, though Sergey Bulgakov, the future Orthodox theologian, emphasized the dogmatism of the atheistic intelligentsia and its imperviousness to critical argument, he also saw in the radical youth 'a certain other-worldliness, an eschatological dream of the City of God and the future reign of justice ... and a striving for the salvation of mankind'.[14] Bulgakov saw the atheism of the Russian radical youth as taking on some of the features of religious faith, 'only inside out'.[15] At the same time he regarded this quasi-religious attitude as manifesting a certain heroism and an anti-philistine spirit.

Vekhi was not a carefully planned monolithic production. But the contributors shared a common general outlook, and certain themes tended to recur. For example, Kistyakovsky had conceived law as protecting human rights, and the radical intelligentsia as lacking any real understanding of the value of the human personality and of the rights belonging to the human being as such. We can add that several of the contributors underlined the need to counterbalance the intelligentsia's concentration of attention on society and social classes by emphasizing the value and freedom of the person. According to Bulgakov, it was precisely the absence of any adequate idea of personality which constituted 'the intelligentsia's chief weakness'.[16] In the minds of its members, Bulgakov argued, the word 'social' possessed a kind of sacred sacramental quality, whereas they had little use for such ideas as those of personal morality and personal self-improvement. Indeed Gerschenzon, in his forthright manner, claimed that what the Russian *intelligent* needed to be told was to 'try to become a human being',[17] a harmoniously and fully developed rather than a split or defective personality. In an essay on the thought of the *Vekhi* group Leonard Schapiro claimed that it was not only Solovyev's 'philosophical idealism' which influenced the contributors to the symposium, but that they also saw in Solovyev's thought 'a revival of the

14. *L*, p. 28

15. *L*, p. 30

16. *L*, p. 44

17. *L*, p. 64

Christian humanism of Erasmus and St Thomas More'.[18] However this may be, they were certainly humanists in the sense that they insisted on the intrinsic value of the human personality; and it is also true that they saw religion as a sure basis for humanism. The readiness of the atheistic and revolutionary intelligentsia to treat human beings, or see them treated, simply as means to the attainment of a social end determined by the *intelligenty* themselves was regarded by the contributors to *Vekhi* as closely linked with their contempt for religion and religious values.

In his essay just mentioned Leonard Schapiro cited Solovyev's 'vision of impending doom'[19] as exercising an influence on the thought of the *Vekhi* group. Schapiro was thinking of the way in which Solovyev, in the closing years of his life, came to expect a world-wide spread of the kingdom of Antichrist, of an atheist regime in which Christians would be reduced to a small and despised minority. For Solovyev, an increasing apostasy would herald the approaching end of history and the coming of divine judgment. To what extent the contributors to *Vekhi* were actually influenced by Solovyev's vision of impending doom seems difficult to determine, but they certainly feared that Russia, polarized between an intransigent political regime on the one hand and a revolutionary and atheistic youth on the other, was heading for disaster. They regarded themselves as morally obliged to do what they could to save Russia from the fate which threatened her. This involved subjecting the ideas of the intelligentsia to criticism; but it was certainly not a question of coming to the defence of the autocracy, while condemning the intelligentsia. It was a question of expounding truths, in the light of which judgment could be passed both on the would-be revolutionaries and on the regime which they wished to overturn. The members of the *Vekhi* group were convinced that a better society could not be realized by following the policy of intensifying oppositions and

18. *Russian Studies*, by Leonard Schapiro, edited by Ellen Dahrendorf, with an Introduction by Harry Willetts, p. 79 (London, 1986). Schapiro's essay on the *Vekhi* group first appeared in December, 1955, in *The Slavonic and East European Review*.

19. *Ibid.*

clashes within the social body to the point of explosion. They did not call for total destruction and a completely new start. In their view, what was needed was a kind of spiritual and moral re-education which could serve as a basis for enlightened action.

II

From one point of view at any rate the publication of *Vekhi* was a great success. In the short period between March 1909 and February 1910 it ran through five editions. Needless to say, to arouse widespread interest is not the same thing as winning widespread acceptance. As has already been noted, the symposium gave rise to furious controversy and evoked counterblasts from various quarters, relatively more polite ones from liberals (including Pavel Milyukov, leader of the Cadets, member of the Constitutional Democratic Party, and a positivist), more abusive ones from the Social Democrats and Socialist Revolutionaries. 'Only with the coming of the war in 1914 did the debate over *Vekhi* come to an end.'[20]

In 1918, after the Bolshevik seizure of power, some of the contributors to *Vekhi*, with the addition of Vyacheslav Ivanov and Pavel Novgorodtsev (editor of *Problems of Idealism*), collaborated, at the suggestion of Peter Struve, in composing another symposium entitled *Out of the Depths (Iz Glubiny, De Profundis)*. Though printed in 1918, the symposium was not published at that time. It was apparently the printers who put some copies on sale in 1921, most of which were confiscated by the authorities. The general line of thought in the work was markedly religious, and, as might be expected, the revolution was regarded as confirming the validity of *Vekhi*'s assessment of the Russian intelligentsia and its leaders.

Even after the Bolshevik seizure of power in November (October Old Style) 1917 there was a certain amount of cultural freedom for a while, if only because the new regime had more pressing tasks to attend to than clamping down on writers and lecturers, not to speak of artists and poets. For example, Berdyaev was able to teach for a time in a 'Free Academy of Spiritual Culture' at Moscow, and in 1920 he became,

20. *L*, p. 65. From a contribution by A. Levin.

rather surprisingly, a professor of philosophy in the university. Again, though Bulgakov was ordained priest in 1918, he was able to remain in academic life for two or three years. Further, in 1922 Izgoev and some colleagues were able to publish a reply to views expressed in *A Change of Landmarks* (*Cmena Vekh*, 1921). The contributors to this work, mostly former Cadets, recommended reconciliation with Bolshevism, whereas Izgoev and his friends insisted on the need to stick to principles.

When, however, the Civil War was over and the regime felt more secure, it turned its attention to establishing a monopoly for the Marxist-Leninist ideology, and in 1922 a large number of scholars and thinkers was expelled from the Soviet Union. Among the exiles were most of the thinkers who had contributed to *Vekhi*. Gerschenzon stayed in Russia, but Berdyaev, Frank, Bulgakov, Kistyakovsky and Izgoev went abroad. The philosopher N.O. Lossky, together with his son Vladimir, was also expelled in 1922. Peter Struve had already left the country.

It is obviously possible to regard the expulsions of 1922 as a cause for rejoicing rather than for lamentation. There were, indeed, one or two unfortunates. Thus Lev Platonovich Karsavin (1882–1952), historian and philosopher, who was one of the expellees, accepted a university chair in Lithuania and, when the Baltic states were annexed by the Soviet Union in the second world war, he was sent to a labour camp where he eventually perished. In most cases, however, expulsion enabled scholars and thinkers to continue their work abroad and publish their writings. If they had remained in their native country, who knows how many of them would have escaped consignment to a labour camp or death during Stalin's purges? In any case the philosophers and religious thinkers would not have been able to publish their works in the Soviet Union. It is true, of course, that the exiled thinkers were cut off from the reading public in their homeland, so that their sphere of influence was greatly curtailed. But they were not reduced to silence, as they would have been if they had remained in the Soviet Union, nor were they unable to exercise some influence. To take but one, and probably the most obvious example, for a time at any rate Berdyaev was a well-known thinker and writer in the West, and nowadays he is by no means unknown in such circles in the Soviet Union. The religious thinkers in exile kept alive a tradition in Russian thought going back through Solovyev to Dostoevsky and Chaadaev.

III

In the contributions to *Vekhi* adverse criticism of the spirit, policies and ideas of the Russian intelligentsia has been a conspicuous, indeed the most conspicuous feature. But if the various writers criticized radical youth and its leaders, this was obviously because they believed that the intelligentsia, imbued with positivism and utilitarianism, which it combined with social ideals, lacked an outlook on reality, a world-view, which could form a basis or framework for the valuable elements in its ideals in a way in which positivism and materialism were quite unable to do. As was remarked above, Bulgakov believed that the chief defect of the intelligentsia was its lack of any adequate concept of human personality and the value of the human person. The religious thinkers among the expellees of 1922—Berdyaev, Frank, Lossky, Karsavin and Bulgakov himself—can be seen as presenting, in their several ways, a religiously-based humanism, a religiously grounded philosophical or theological anthropology. In 1909, the year of *Vekhi*'s publication, they had been primarily concerned with trying to make it clear to the radical intelligentsia that, so far from leading the nation into the Promised Land, it was pursuing or advocating courses of action which could only do great harm to Russia. After the events of 1917 the contributors to *Vekhi* saw their worst fears confirmed, and the lesson was underlined in *De Profundis* in 1918. After 1922, however, the religious thinkers in exile, instead of spending their time in recrimination and repeating 'I told you so', devoted their attention to more positive and constructive work, developing religiously oriented philosophical thought or, in the case of Father Bulgakov, pursuing theological speculation with the aid of philosophical ideas.

Regarded in the light of their relationship to Vladimir Solovyev, the work of the Russian religious thinkers might be described in this sort of way. Reference was made above to the sense of urgency, of theatening disaster, which was felt by the contributors to *Vekhi*. There were plenty of grounds for this feeling without bringing in Solovyev. But if, with Schapiro, we choose to see in this sense of urgency an analogy with the vision of impending doom experienced by Solovyev in his last years, this is obviously not altogether unreasonable, for the Russian intelligentsia can perfectly well be seen as disseminating the atheism and contempt for religion which Solovyev conceived in terms of the growth of the reign of Antichrist. For most of his adult life, however, Solovyev was engaged in trying to fulfil what he saw as the need for a systematically developed religious world-view, a general interpretation of the world and of human life and history from within the sphere of Christian faith. The Russian religious thinkers who were exiled in 1922 can be seen as having contributed in their several ways to the fulfilment of this ongoing task. Their lines of thought were by no means all the same. For example, Frank was much more sympathetic than Lossky was, let alone Berdyaev, to Solovyev's emphasis on the metaphysical idea of total-unity, the idea of the Absolute, which Lossky, and still more Berdyaev, saw as threatening genuine recognition of the freedom of the human being. Again, Frank and Lossky were both more given to systematic philosophical reflection and argument than was Berdyaev who proclaimed his visions and was not much concerned with either argumentation or consistency, let alone with creating a system. Systems of philosophy he mistrusted, but he was a great champion of freedom and a resolute opponent of all collectivism or totalitarianism, metaphysical or social-political. In spite, however, of their differences we can reasonably regard all of the exiled Russian religious philosophers as being, in their several ways, spiritual heirs of Solovyev.

IV

It is natural to assume that the thinkers who have been described as Solovyev's spiritual heirs came upon the scene too late, at any rate as far as Russia was concerned. Writing to Sergey Diaghilev at the end of December 1902, Anton Chekhov remarked that 'as for the educated segment of our society, it appears to have departed from religion and to be going further and further away from it, no matter what is said and what kind of philosophico-religious associations may be formed'.[21] Chekhov was not himself a religious believer, but he was reporting what he judged to be happening in Russian society. In the letter in

21. Yarmolinsky, p. 438. See note 13 above.

question he seems to understand by 'the educated segment of society' something considerably wider than revolutionary youth and its leaders. After all, the alienation of the radical intelligentsia could be taken for granted. It is thus reasonable to assume that Chekhov was referring to a growing indifference to religion among educated and reflective Russians who were certainly not propagandists for revolution.

Chekhov was not alone, of course, in viewing the situation in this way and if we assume that his remarks were justified, it is natural to ask whether the efforts made by Solovyev's spiritual heirs to recall their fellow countrymen to a religiously oriented world-view were not too late and foredoomed to failure. True, in *Vekhi* there was no obvious recall to religion in a traditional sense; emphasis on the need for religious faith was much clearer in *Iz Glubiny* or *De Profundis*. But as this second work was composed after the Bolshevik seizure of power had taken place, it may seem that emphasis on the need for religion expressed what might be described as a counsel of despair, as though nothing was left but to take refuge in religious faith and hopes. As for the religious thinkers who were expelled from the Soviet Union in 1922, if they really hoped to exercise an influence on the minds of their fellow countrymen, must we not look on this hope as a case of unwarranted optimism, at any rate once the Bolshevik leaders had consolidated their power and eliminated all potentially effective opposition? To be sure, Berdyaev made a name for himself in the West as an interpreter of events in Russia and of the significance of these events for world-history; Frank and N.O. Lossky became respected philosophers; and Bulgakov was a leading Orthodox theologian, resident in Paris for a good many years. As far, however, as the Soviet Union was concerned, after 1922 were not these men, described as spiritual heirs of Solovyev, unable to exercise even the very limited degree of influence which Solovyev himself had been able to exercise in nineteenth-century Tsarist Russia?

This way of regarding the situation is understandable. Further, it is obviously based on fact. At the same time there are other considerations which should be borne in mind. Consider, for example, the publication of *Vekhi* in 1909. Looking back on this event in later years Semyon Frank emphasized that the work had a specific purpose, namely to subject to critical analysis what he described as the sacred dogmas of the intelligentsia. This, of course, it did, and in an outspoken manner. The contributors did not claim that they themselves had always occupied positions which were beyond justifiable attack. Berdyaev, writing as one who had once experienced the lure of Marxism, asserted that 'our approach to philosophy was just as shallow as our approach to other spiritual values; we denied the autonomous significance of philosophy and subordinated it to utilitarian social goals'.[22] In other words, thinkers such as Berdyaev, who had previously belonged to the radical intelligentsia, believed that they had come to see the light, and they wished to facilitate a similar awakening on the part of any member of the intelligentsia who was prepared to consider criticism seriously. It is obviously true that there is a real sense in which the criticism levelled by *Vekhi* came too late. But it by no means follows that its publication was a waste of time, if this is implied. For one thing, in the ensuing controversy some minds at any rate were influenced by *Vekhi*, even if the general reaction of the intelligentsia was strongly negative. For another thing, the work provides a lasting proof that the power of self-criticism was not simply dead among the educated Russian youth of the time, and that some representatives of youth at any rate were able to see and draw forcible attention to the dangerous attitudes and lines of thought adopted and promoted by the Russian intelligentsia, such as readiness to sacrifice individual living human beings in the name of some abstract ideal or of generations yet unborn and to consider any means justified by whatever social goal the intelligentsia might have accepted. What is more, although *Vekhi* was published only five years before the outbreak of the war which contributed powerfully to the fall of the regime and the triumph of the Bolshevik leaders, it had by no means lost all its relevance. Soviet students, for instance, could very well profit from taking to heart some of the lessons taught by *Vekhi*. The work was, of course, written in a different historical situation and for a different readership; but much of what was said in it had a validity which is not confined to the circumstances of 1909.

As for the books and articles published abroad by the expellees of 1922, if we understand 'arriving in time' in the present context as implying free sale and dissemination by means of the bookshops,

22. *L*, p. 4

universities and higher educational institutes of the Soviet Union, it hardly needs saying that the books and articles in question arrived too late. But there are two points to bear in mind. First, the works of thinkers such as Berdyaev, Bulgakov, Frank and Lossky helped to keep alive the traditions of Russian religious thought in Russian circles outside the Soviet Union. Secondly, the writings of the religious thinkers expelled in 1922 are not simply unknown objects for inhabitants of the USSR. In one way or another knowledge of the thought of writers such as Berdyaev and Bulgakov has increased in the Soviet Union and has awakened a lively interest in receptive minds. Needless to say, the number of people interested in religious philosophy and in Orthodox theology is limited. There is nothing new in this. But it does not alter the fact that, by penetrating limited circles within the Soviet Union, Russian religious thought is kept alive and a bridge is established between the old Russia and the Russia which is gradually coming into being. The works of Russian religious thinkers in exile were certainly not written in vain. For a time they helped to enrich thought in Europe and America. And in recent years they have stimulated interest and reflection in the homeland of those who died in exile.

V

In the first section of this chapter attention was drawn to the fact that, in order to counterbalance the radical intelligentsia's preoccupation with revolutionary action (and the liberals' preoccupation with constitutional and economic reform), the contributors to *Vekhi* insisted on the need for an inner conversion, a real *metanoia*, a change in consciousness. That is to say, whereas the leaders of the intelligentsia talked as though realization of the social-political structural changes which they considered desirable would automatically produce a desired change of consciousness, the contributors to *Vekhi* insisted that it was folly to suppose that overthrow of the existing regime would bring about a kind of miraculous transformation of human society for the better. What was needed was that people should set about changing themselves for the better.

This sort of attitude on the part of the contributors to *Vekhi* had brought upon them as we noted, the accusation that they wanted only peace and order and, in effect, supported the existing regime, blinding themselves to the obvious need for change. On behalf of the symposiasts we replied that this accusation was unjust, and that the authors of *Vekhi* had no intention of condemning all change and of supporting the claims of the autocracy. But by way of conclusion to this chapter I wish to say a little more about this theme.

At the end of the first chapter reference was made to the paper which in 1891 Solovyev read to a society in Moscow and in which he made clear his conviction that unbelievers, in campaigning for the remedying of obvious social evils, had been carrying on a work which had been shamefully neglected by the official representatives of Orthodox Christianity, the very people who should have manifested a genuine social concern. In his ethical work *The Justification of the Good* he insisted that it was the business of the state to create for all citizens the conditions required for leading a decent human life and for developing their gifts. As a man who had no use for *Realpolitik* and who claimed that rulers and politicians were by no means exempt from the moral law, even in their public capacities, he was certainly not disposed to encourage governmental indifference to exploitation or oppression of any kind. And if the contributors of *Vekhi* had adopted an attitude of indifference to all matters of social-political reform, they could hardly be described as spiritual heirs of Solovyev.

If the contributors to *Vekhi* devoted themselves to criticism of the intelligentsia, this was because they recognized the great practical importance of the intelligentsia in the life of Russia. The intelligentsia was, so to speak, the spearhead of change. Without it there would be drift or stagnation, punctuated by sporadic peasant insurrection. Any organized policy of change would be the product of members of the intelligentsia. But, in the eyes of the *Vekhi* symposiasts, the revolutionary intelligentsia in particular was heading for disaster. For example, it was lunacy to suppose that appeals to class hatred would produce a society transformed for the better. The revolutionary intelligentsia was preparing the way for the advent of a new and probably more efficient and ruthless dictatorship. Hence the vital importance of trying to bring about, before it was too late, a change of outlook. As Bulgakov put it, 'in order to renovate Russia, it is necessary first of all to renovate ...her intelligentsia'.[23]

This attitude obviously does not rule out all concern with social-political reform. It was a question, as we have remarked before, of putting first things first. Thus Berdyaev emphasized respect for truth, while Frank dwelt more on recognition of objective moral values. As for ideas about social organization, the contributors to *Vekhi* developed them at at later date, in the framework of their religiously oriented world-views, as, indeed, Solovyev had done before them.

This means that different emphases in the various general outlooks were reflected in or accompanied by differences in social-political ideas. Philosophers such as Frank, who stood close to Solovyev in emphasizing the idea of total-unity, the Absolute, naturally laid stress on social unity and on the duty of society to care for its members. Thus when Frank came to write about the matter, he argued that society should ideally exemplify the concept of *sobornost*, of 'togetherness'. Togetherness, organic unity, should, he maintained, constitute the inner layer of society, its soul. Every society, however, required an outer layer of 'externality', represented, in the case of the state, by such factors as law. It was Frank's conviction that maintenance of the inner spirit of *sobornost* required an external organization, the aim of which should be to preserve and promote the spirit of unity, of togetherness. Political authorities were certainly not morally free to turn a blind eye on social injustice or on the exploitation of one section of the population by another. It is true that Frank was primarily interested in metaphysics and philosophy of religion, but he also wrote on themes relating to social philosophy, his most substantial work in this field being *The Spiritual Foundations of Society*, which appeared in 1930.[24]

Solovyev's idea of total-unity seemed to Berdyaev to smack of monism, and monism, whether cosmic or social (in the form of collectivism, that is to say) was abhorrent to a thinker who proclaimed

23. *L*, p. 26

24. In 1922 Frank had published an *Essay on the Methodology of the Social Sciences*.

his belief in 'the supremacy of personality over society'.[25] Though, however, Berdyaev's enthusiastic love of freedom and his respect for personality (assisted, some would urge, by an aristocratic attitude) led him on occasion to speak of the state in thoroughly derogatory terms, he admitted, perhaps rather grudgingly, that it was a necessary institution in life and that it possessed a 'functional importance'.[26]

Its principal function, he maintained, was to see that there were no hungry people, no unemployed, no exploitation of man by man.[27] Berdyaev was a convinced enemy of collectivism and totalitarianism, but he did not attack these targets out of any love for capitalism. He strongly objected to Christianity being used to defend the capitalist system, which he described as 'a religion of the Golden Calf'.[28] As against collectivist socialism on the one hand and capitalism on the other he advocated what he described as personalist socialism, 'the social projection of personalism'.[29] To be sure, he left the nature of this socialism pretty vague. But it is at any rate clear that, while his respect for the freedom and value of the human person as such inspired him with a hatred of collectivism, this same respect for the person led him to condemn all forms of oppression and exploitation masquerading under the name of non-interference with individual liberty.

It can hardly be denied that the writing of at any rate the more metaphysically minded of the Russian religious philosophers tends to appear very tame in comparison with the impassioned utterances of leaders of pre-1917 revolutionary intelligentsia. The latter were writing with a view to action, subordinating all other considerations (moral, for example) to the furtherance of their social goals, whereas the former,

---

25. *Slavery and Freedom*, translated by R.M. French, p. 17 (London, 1944). This translation will be referred to in notes as *SF*.

26. *The Beginning and the End*, translated by R.M. French, p. 217 (London, 1952). This translation will be referred to in notes as *BE*.

27. *SF*, p. 150

28. *Dream and Reality. An Essay in Autobiography*, translated by K. Lampert, p. 212 (London, 1950). This translation will be referred to in notes as *DR*.

29. *DR*, p. 17

philosophizing quietly in their places of exile abroad, were well aware that their chances of exercising any effective influence on the course of events in their homeland were slight. But the fact that they philosophized rather than issued clarion calls for drastic action does not show that they were indifferent to hopes for the transformation of society for the better. And much of what they wrote about the nature and organization of human society has retained its relevance, a relevance which is not confined to their own native land.

Chapter 3

Philosophy of history

In 1919–20, when the new regime was still too preoccupied with other matters to have got around to a systematic elimination of all public expression of ideas at variance with its own ideology, Berdyaev gave a series of lectures at Moscow which formed the basis for his work *The Meaning of History*, the Russian text of which appeared at Berlin in 1923.[1] In his brief foreward to this volume he asserts that, in the nineteenth century, philosophical thought in Russia was mainly concerned with problems in the philosophy of history. He goes on to claim that for Chaadaev and the Slavophiles 'the enigma of Russia and of her historical destiny was synonymous with that of the philosophy of history'.[2] Finally he maintains that philosophical thought in Russia has had the specific mission of developing a religious philosophy of history.

The first two claims are descriptive. In regard to the first, it is clearly true that the theme of history was a prominent feature of philosophical thought in Russia during the nineteenth century. For example, Apollon Grigoryev (1822–64) criticized Hegel's idea of history as one overall process of dialectical advance and argued that each nation could be likened to a biological organism which develops according to its own laws. This theory was further developed by Nikolai Danilevsky (1822–85) who discerned in history up-to-date ten distinct types of civilization, each of which evolved according to its own immanent principles or laws, even though, in a manner analogous to that in which one biological organism can assimilate material derived from another,

1. There is an English translation by George Reavey (London, 1936). This will be referred to in notes as *MH*.

2. *MH*, p. vii

37

it is possible for one civilization to enrich itself with material derived from another. The analogy of a biological organism was also employed by Konstantin Leontyev (1831–1914), who represented each society or civilization as passing, in the course of its normal development,[3] through a succession of stages, namely growth, maturity, decay and death. Between them, Danilevsky and Leontyev anticipated the sort of ideas expounded by the German scholar Oswald Spengler in his *The Decline of the West*, which appeared in 1918.

Leo Tolstoy was not, of course, a professional philosopher; but if one is thinking of examples of reflection on problems in the philosophy of history in nineteenth-century Russia, the name of the great novelist can hardly fail to come to mind. As anyone who has succeeded in reading the whole of *War and Peace* is well aware, the author devotes the second part of the Epilogue to a discussion of historiography and the philosophy of history. Tolstoy is doubtless best known for the way in which he minimizes the historical importance and role of those prominent persons whom Hegel described as 'world-historical individuals', people such as the Emperor Napoleon I. Tolstoy was not however, concerned simply with belittling the leader of the forces which had invaded Russia. He discussed, for example, causal explanation in history and the question whether (and, if so, how) historiography could become a science. But it would be inappropriate to examine these theories here.[4]

Berdyaev's second assertion, namely that for Chaadaev and the Slavophiles the problem of Russia's destiny was the central problem of the philosophy of history, is certainly true in a sense. Chaadaev, as Berdyaev was obviously well aware, was not a Slavophile as this term is generally understood by historians. Whereas he believed that old Russia had nothing of value to offer the world and therefore regarded Peter the Great's opening to the West as an inestimable blessing for his country, a

3. 'Normal'. Leontyev had, of course, to allow for such possible events as premature termination of a society's life by natural catastrophe or conquest by another society.

4. See Sir Isaiah Berlin's essay *The Hedgehog and the Fox*, which is reprinted in *Russian Thinkers* (London, 1979). There is a treatment of Tolstoy's ideas about history in the present writer's *Philosophy in Russia*, pp. 180–5 (Tunbridge Wells, 1986).

step on a road which it was highly desirable that Russia should travel, the Slavophiles (some more than others) deplored the influence of the West on Holy Mother Russia and tended to paint a rosy picture of pre-Petrine Russia. But in spite of their different convictions both Chaadaev and the Slavophiles focused their attention on problems relating to the destiny and role in human history of their own nation. Whether they would have been prepared to claim that the problem of Russia and the philosophy of history were identical, is another question. But it would be a mistake to interpret Berdyaev as implying that this is what they thought. What he says is that by their concentration on the theme of Russia's role in human history Chaadaev and the Slavophiles helped to stimulate reflection on problems in the speculative philosophy of history. And this is doubtless quite true.

We can see Danilevsky and Leontyev as widening the field and placing the theme of Russia's destiny in a broad context, namely the idea of a plurality of societies or civilizations each of which comes into being, grows and matures, decays and dies. As mentioned, Danilevsky believed that he had identified in history the historico-cultural types of civilization. He added, however, that Russia's destiny was to create an eleventh type, Slav civilization. So Russia had her place in his scheme. But as the various types of civilization or society were said to develop independently, each according to its own immanent laws or principles, one could hardly see history as one process of development, looking foward to Russia's contribution. At the same time, by allowing that one society may derive material from another Danilevsky seems to have left room for the contention that Slav society had derived so much material from other types of civilization—such as, in particular, western Europe—that it would count as the richest. In point of fact Danilevsky did hold that when Russia had conquered Constantinople and had brought together all Slav peoples under her hegemony, the resulting society would come nearer than any other to realizing the ideal of a universal human society. How this belief about the future fits in with Danilevsky's idea of distinct societies developing according to their several immanent laws is not altogether easy to see. But he did his best to combine with this idea the allocation to Russia of a kind of world-mission.

As for Berdyaev's third claim, it is expressed in a perhaps somewhat ambiguous manner. When he refers to the development of a religious philosophy of history as the specific mission of Russian philosophical thought, it is natural to assume that he is making a normative statement, asserting what, in his judgment, Russian philosophy should be or what should be its distinguishing characteristic. But what he actually says is that development of a religious philosophy of history seems or appears to be the specific mission of Russian philosophical thought, and the reason which Berdyaev gives for saying this is that Russian philosophy has always shown a predilection for the eschatological problem and apocalypticism. It is thus possible to understand him as making a purely descriptive statement about philosophical thought in Russia, namely that it seems to have centred round problems relating to the goal or meaning of history. Given, however, Berdyaev's own predilection for discussing the goal or end of history, it seems reasonable to interpret his statement in the foreword to *The Meaning of History* as being partly descriptive and partly normative.

Considered as descriptive, Berdyaev's statement is a not unreasonable generalization, especially if we bear in mind his use of terms such as 'philosophy' and 'philosopher'. For example, although Dostoevsky was certainly not a professional philosopher and would be judged by some people to have been innocent of anything which could justifiably be described as philosophical thought, Berdyaev regarded him as much more deserving of the epithet 'philosopher' than many professional philosophers. However this may be, Dostoevsky certainly offered a general interpretation of human history in terms of a struggle between those engaged in trying to realize the kingdom of God in the world and those trying to establish the kingdom of Man to the exclusion of God, between the followers of the God-man and the followers of the Man-God, and he liked to ascribe a special mission and role to Russia in the movement of history.

The objection can obviously be raised that, though Danilevsky and Leontyev pursued speculative philosophy of history, what they produced were naturalistic rather than religious theories. Similarly, though the Populist writers Peter Lavrov (1823–1900), Peter Tkachev (1844–86) and Nikolai Mikhailovsky (1842–1904) expounded theories relating to history, they were not religious believers. If Berdyaev meant to imply that nineteenth-century Russian philosophical thought in general took the form of religiously oriented philosophy of history, either he was mistaken or he was refusing to regard as philosophers people who had at any rate as much right as Dostoevsky to being so described.

It is perhaps worth noting that, though Leontyev's theory of history was, in itself, a naturalistic theory, as was Danilevsky's, Leontyev was or rather became a deeply religious man, undergoing a religious conversion and dying as a monk. But he drew a sharp distinction between social organisms and persons. The former, he maintained, develop and decay according to certain laws; they are not persons; they are not subject to moral judgment, as persons are; and the claim that human history exemplifies a continuous advance and will see the realization of an earthly paradise (which Leontyev accused Dostoevsky, Tolstoy and Solovyev of claiming—he was not referring to Solovyev's later expectations, of course) is certainly not warranted by Christian belief. Whatever we may think of this line of thought, it might perhaps be described as being, in its own way, a religious view of history. Leontyev certainly thought about history as a Christian.

Leontyev apart, however, it can reasonably be argued that in generalizing about the nature of nineteenth-century philosophical thought in Russia Berdyaev focused his attention too much on a certain tradition as being genuinely Russian and not the result of western influence or the imitation of western models. But is has already been admitted that when Berdyaev wrote about the development of a religious philosophy of history as being the specific mission of Russian philosophical thought and as a feature which distinguished Russian from western thought, his statements can justifiably be interpreted as being partly normative, as expressing what Berdyaev thought ought to be the case or what he considered appropriate to Russian tradition and wanted to be the case. After all, Berdyaev had for a while been a Marxist, and one of the features of Marxism which had attracted him in the first instance, and which he continued to regard as representing the better side, so to speak, of Marxist theory, was its wide view of history and its freedom, as he saw it, from the narrow provincial outlook of 'Russian socialism'. Marx looked forward to the eventual realization of a world-wide human society, and he provided man with a goal, with something to strive after and sacrifice himself for. To be sure, the Marxist ideology was atheistic. But this was obviously a feature of Marxism which stimulated Berdyaev to insist on the need for a religiously oriented interpretation of history to counterbalance that of Marx. We should also bear in mind the fact that the lectures which formed the basis for *The Meaning of History* were delivered after the Bolshevik seizure of power, after the triumph of a Party inspired by a materialistic and atheistic world-view. Berdyaev was very naturally convinced of the importance of presenting an alternative vision of reality, a religiously inspired interpretation of the world and of human life and history. It was his conviction at the time of the lectures that the Russian revolution had ushered in a new era and that when what had seemed stable was tottering, problems relating to the nature and goal of history and the significance of human life and activity were bound to come to the fore in human consciousness.

II

Let us return to Vladimir Solovyev, the foremost Russian speculative philosopher of the nineteenth century. In comparison with Russia at the time when Berdyaev was giving his lectures at Moscow on the meaning of history, Solovyev's Russia must have seemed a relatively stable society. To be sure, in 1881 Alexander II, the Tsar-Liberator, was assassinated by representatives of the People's Will group (a terrorist offshoot of the Populist movement), and Solovyev was obviously well aware not only that there was fairly widespread dissatisfaction with the regime but also that under the surface there were groups which hoped for and planned revolution. But after the murder of Alexander II, his successor, Alexander III, and his government took a firm line, and any successful attempt at revolution must have seemed, as indeed it was at the time, a very remote possibility. Solovyev did not live to witness the revolution of 1905–06, let alone the first world war and the dramatic events of 1917. Perhaps it is not altogether fanciful to suggest that in nineteenth-century Russia it was considerably easier for him to develop an elaborate and abstruse metaphysics, which calls to mind the thought of the German idealists, than it would have been in the years immediately following the Bolsheviks' seizure of power, when the future of Russia still hung in the balance.

Though theory of knowledge and metaphysics were prominent features of Solovyev's thought, it by no means follows that he passed over or neglected social-political thought and philosophy of history. He did not neglect such themes, but there are discernible connections between his treatment of them and the more abstract parts of his philosophy. Whereas Berdyaev mistrusted systems and had no ambition to add to their number, in Solovyev's thought the movement towards systematization and synthesis was strongly marked.

In his metaphysics Solovyev presented what amounts to a philosophical version of the Christian doctrine of the Trinity. God, the ultimate reality, was conceived not as an undifferentiated unity but as a unity comprising three distinct hypostases. In other words, Solovyev attributed to God or the Absolute (he assumed that the terms could be used interchangeably) a social aspect. It is not possible to pursue here a critical discussion of Solovyev's treatment of the inner life of the Deity. The point which I wish to make is that his philosophical deduction of the Trinity affects his view of the created world. For the inner life of the Godhead is depicted as expressing itself externally in creation. Unity does not disappear in the process of creation, for the world is a whole of interrelated beings. At the same time creation involves the appearance of distinct individual beings, each of which is capable, at any rate at a certain level of evolution, of trying to preserve itself at the expense of others. Human beings in particular can and do oppose one another. It hardly needs saying that creation has meant the emergence of egoism, tribal wars, enmity between nations and classes. Indeed, Solovyev does not hesitate to assert that 'every creature, from a grain of dust to a man, is out only to affirm itself: I alone exist, and everything else exists only for me'.[5] At the same time unity does not entirely disappear, for the human being is by nature a social being, in the sense that each needs other human beings and cannot become a fully developed person without them. On occasion Solovyev speaks in a way which puts one in mind of Karl Marx. For example, he asserts that 'each individual is only

5. *God, Man and the Church: The Spiritual Foundations of Life*, translated by Donald Attwater, p. 92 (London, undated).

the meeting-point of an infinite number of relations with other individuals'.[6]

Under the influence of thinkers such as Schelling, Solovyev spoke of
creation as a cosmic fall from unity, a fall manifested by the emergence
of egoistic, warring individuals. What was required was a recovery of
unity, and in spite of the emergence of egoism the fact that the human
being is and remains a social being by nature makes this recovery
possible. Solovyev insisted, however, that restoration of unity does not
entail the disappearance of all distinctions and the merging of the Many
in an undifferentiated One. After all, though from one point of view
creation was a fall, it also expressed or manifested the Godhead, the
inner life of which can be described as social. Hence an overcoming of
egoism and separation and a return to unity on the part of human
beings would mean realization of a universal society of men and women
united with God and one another. A society of this kind, says Solovyev,
is what is meant by the kingdom of God. And its realization is the goal
of history.

Did Solovyev believe that the perfect and universal society which he
identified with the kingdom of God would eventually be realized on
earth, within history? For a long time he doubtless thought that, as God
works in history, things would get better rather than worse. And there
are passages which suggest the idea of inevitability. Thus Solovyev
referred to Buddhism and Platonism as 'necessary stages of human
consciousness',[7] a statement which recalls to mind the ideas of Hegel.
At the same time he can hardly have believed that the kingdom of God
could be fully realized on earth, in historical time. For realization of a
completely universal human society would require resurrection of the
dead. Though Solovyev doubtless sympathized with the claim made by
Nikolai Fyodorov (1828–1903) that fidelity to the spirit of human
brotherhood demands concern for the departed, he does not seem to
have shared Fyodorov's eccentric notion that scientists should set about
finding the means of bringing 'our fathers' back to life in this world. In

6. *The Justification of the Good. An Essay on Moral Philosophy*, translated by
   Nathalie A. Duddington, p. 199 (London, 1918). This work will be referred to in
   notes as *JG*.

7. *Ibid.*, p. 246

any case, as has already been mentioned, in his later years Solovyev became acutely conscious of the prevalence and power of evil and envisaged the advent of the reign of Antichrist, with Christians being reduced to a small minority and with reunion of the Churches under the Pope taking place just before the curtain is rung down on life in this world. None the less, realization of the kingdom of God remained for him the goal of history, even if this goal could be fully realized only beyond history.

Solovyev did not simply say that the goal of history is the realization of a perfect society and leave the matter there. He went on to describe this society as a divine-human organism. The divine element, we are told, has its collective expression in the Church, which will eventually 'include all mankind and all nature in one universal theandric organism'.[8] (When action proceeds from God and the human being together, Solovyev calls the action 'theandric'.) The human element in the divine-human organism has its collective expression in the state. As for the bond between the two elements, this is said to be 'a free union of Church and state'[9], when, that is to say, the latter has taken the form of the Christian state.

At first therefore Solovyev looked forward to the realization of a theocratic society, an ideal which he expounded in his work *History and Future of Theocracy*. It is an ideal which can easily be misunderstood. In the first place Solovyev explicitly asserts that he does not intend to identify the Church, considered as the expression of the divine element in the divine-human organism, with 'historical Christianity or the visible Church (which one?)'.[10] In this context the Church should be understood as meaning the one mystical Body of Christ, which cannot be identified with any particular religious body existing here and now. In the second place Solovyev rejects any claim that the Church has a right to exercise coercion, even over its own members, let alone those who are not its members.[11] Nor did he maintain that the Church should

8. *God, Man and the Church*, p. 136

9. *Ibid.*, p. 174

10. *JG*, p. 194, note I.

11. *Ibid.*, p. 265

use the state as an instrument of coercion. What he had in mind, as he insisted, was a 'free' theocracy. This, he at first maintained, was the ideal goal of history, something to the realization of which he called on human beings to contribute voluntarily in their several ways. Whether or not we are prepared to regard realization of such an ideal as a practical possibility is another question. After all, Solovyev himself came to have serious doubts, as far as this world was concerned.

Sometimes Solovyev makes statements which, taken by themselves, naturally tend to confirm the worst fears of a suspicious reader. A prize example is the statement that 'the state must be the political organ of the Church'.[12] What Solovyev means can be expressed in this way. The Church seeks or ought to seek realization of the kingdom of God. But this goal cannot be attained by the efforts of the Church alone. For the kingdom of God cannot be realized on earth, so far as this realization is possible, without a genuine and active concern for social justice or without regulation of economic conditions. The Church, however, is not in position to regulate economic life or ensure, for example, that the workers enjoy the means for leading decent and full human lives. The cooperation of the state is obviously required, and it can be described as a Christian state in so far as it contributes, in its own appropriate ways, to the development of the perfect society. To claim that the state should serve as the political organ of the Church is not to say that it should serve the particular interests of this or that ecclesiastical hierarchy or religious body. Solovyev firmly believed that political rulers and politicians are subject to the same moral law as other people, not only in their private lives but also when acting in their public capacities. Realization of a free theocracy would mean among other things, that the state would be guided by Christian principles and values. This is what Solovyev understood by a Christian state. As far as he was concerned, religious coercion or repression was not a Christian principle.

For a time Solovyev liked to think that the Slav peoples, and Russia in particular, were especially qualified and called by God to promote the process which, ideally, would culminate in realization of a world-wide

---

12. *Russia and the Universal Church*, translated by Herbert Rees, p. 204 (London, 1948).

free theocracy, uniting all mankind. As we have had occasion to remark, however, in his last years he came to envisage the advent not of a world-wide theocracy but rather of a world-wide empire hostile to Christ but providing mankind with material goods. This development was presented as a possibility rather than as something inevitable. But it is clear that the possibility was seriously entertained, and that Solovyev had called in question his earlier optimistic hopes.[13] If he had lived to witness the events of 1917, he might have seen confirmation of his fears. At the same time he would have insisted that a truly human world-wide society cannot be based on atheism and on the treatment of human beings as expendable means to a social-political end.

It was claimed above that Solovyev's philosophy of history and his social-political theory were closely connected with his metaphysics. This is, I think, clearly true. But Solovyev's talk about unity, fragmentation and return to unity may give rise to a question which was put by the Russian philosopher Leon Shestov, namely whether it is not 'man's task, whatever the ancients may say, not to return to the original "One" but to move as far away from it as possible?'[14] When Shestov asked this question, he was actually thinking of Plotinus and Spinoza, but some readers of Solovyev might want to ask the same question. It is therefore worth reminding ourselves that, although Solovyev saw the root of evil in human life in individualistic self-assertion to the exclusion of concern with others, he also insisted that there cannot be a genuine unity of all, if the all have ceased to exist. 'That each should be destroyed by the whole is no better than that each should try to destroy the others.'[15]

III

Of all the spiritual heirs of Solovyev it is doubtless Berdyaev whose name is particularly associated with reflection on the philosophy of

13. According to his nephew, in the last year or so of his life Solovyev experienced several 'visions' of the devil or principle of evil.

14. *In Job's Balances*, translated by Camilla Coventry and C.A. Macartney p. 173 (London, 1932).

15. *SS*, IX, p. 95. From *Theoretical Philosophy*, I, 4.

history. True, he was not the only one to discuss themes relating to human history, Semyon Frank and Lev Karsavin, for example, did so. But both thinkers are probably better known for their metaphysics (akin to that of Solovyev), whereas it is philosophy of history which the name of Berdyaev brings to mind. Some people might prefer to talk about theology in this connection. To be sure, Berdyaev regarded himself as a philosopher, not as a theologian, and he was certainly not a professional theologian. At the same time it is understandable that when Cambridge conferred on him an honorary degree in 1947, it gave him a doctorate in divinity. The Russian thinker was obviously a committed Christian, and his religious beliefs clearly affected his philosophizing. For example, like Solovyev he regarded the goal of history as realization of the kingdom of God. If it is assumed that philosophy should be free from religious presuppositions, it is not altogether surprising if the conclusion is drawn that Berdyaev's qualifications for being described as a philosopher are questionable, and that a doctorate in divinity would be the appropriate honour. But there can be different ideas of philosophy and we have seen how Kireevsky, Khomyakov, and then Solovyev emphasized the need for philosophical reflection within, so to speak, the area of religious faith. Though Berdyaev's thought differed in important respects from that of Solovyev, it is reasonable to look on him as a committed Christian philosopher, even if he explicitly claimed, and not without reason, that he was not an Orthodox theologian.

In his book *The Beginning and the End* Berdyaev makes what at first sight seems to be a very strange statement, namely that 'the philosophy of history is not merely knowledge of the past, it is also knowledge of the future'.[16] In support of his statement he refers to the Bible, St Augustine, Hegel, Saint-Simon, Auguste Comte and Karl Marx. What he means is evidently that philosophy of history, as distinct from historiography, tries to give meaning to history, that this involves representing it as a movement towards a goal of some kind, and that meaning in this sense cannot be attributed to history without a claim to knowledge of the future being made or implied, the knowledge in

16. *BE*, p. 199

question being knowledge not of particular future historical events but of an ultimate goal or end.

The objection can obviously be raised that, even if philosophy of history as Berdyaev understands it involves no more than a claim to know the future, he has no good reason for asserting that philosophy of history actually is knowledge of the future. It seems to me, however, that we ought not to press the wording of this assertion. In the very same chapter in which Berdyaev says that philosophy of history is knowledge of the future he states that it has always included 'a prophetic element which has passed beyond the bounds of scientific knowledge'[17], and that meaning cannot be given to history unless it covers 'the *unknown* future' (italics mine).[18] Speculative philosophy of history takes its knowledge of the past from historians, but it cannot receive from them knowledge of an unknown future. If therefore the philosopher is to depict the historical process as a movement towards realization of some end or goal, he cannot help acting as a prophet. The prophet's utterance goes beyond the limits of scientific knowledge; but it does not necessarily follow that no reasonable case can be presented for making the prophecy. Thus a claim to knowledge of the movement of history towards a certain end might be based on the belief that there are laws which determine the general movement of history. Or it might be based on the belief that a God who can neither deceive nor be deceived has revealed to mankind through some accredited channel that the historical process is destined to culminate in the attainment of a certain goal. Berdyaev did not believe that there are laws which determine the course of history. He was far too devoted to the idea of human freedom to accept the notion of historical inevitability. His conception of the ideal society, the kingdom of God, was formed in accordance with his interpretation of the human personality, its potentialities and needs; and his confidence that the ideal society would eventually be realized, beyond historical time, was a matter of Christian faith.

17. *Ibid.*

18. *Ibid.*

These last remarks about the development of Berdyaev's idea of the ideal society, the kingdom of God, need some amplification. Berdyaev laid great emphasis on the value of personality and on the human being's freedom and creativeness. He asserted, for example, that 'man, human personality, is the supreme value'.[19] Again, 'man is the dominating idea of my life—man's image, his creative freedom'.[20] Given this sort of value-judgment, Berdyaev was obviously opposed to any policy of treating human beings as nothing but expendable means to the attainment of some ulterior goal. When he spoke of Kant with great respect as 'a profoundly Christian thinker',[21] what he had in mind was the German philosopher's doctrine that a human being should never be treated simply and solely as a means. If, however, history is conceived as a movement towards a goal which will be certainly attained in this world, and if the goal is conceived as an ideal and world-wide society, does it not follow that the members of each successive generation must be regarded as means to the attainment of an end in which they will not share (or only for a short while)? Suppose, for the sake of argument, that history is a process which will culminate in the realization of an ideal universal society in the year 5000 AD. In this case all human beings who were alive in that year would become members of the society, as long as they lived, that is to say. But previous generations would never share in the ideal society, they would be simply means, Berdyaev argued, to the attainment of a goal in which they would never participate. Indeed, each successive generation, including the one alive in 5000 AD would have to be regarded as a means to the welfare of its successor. In Berdyaev's view, this would deprive history of meaning. 'It is only the resurrection of all that have lived which can impart meaning to the historical process of the world, a meaning, that is, which is commensurable with the destiny of personality'.[22]

It follows, of course, that if the goal of history can be realized at all, it can be fully realized only beyond historical time, beyond life in this world. To be sure, realization of the kingdom of God can and does

19. *SF*, p. 28

20. *Solitude and Society*, translated by George Reavey, p. 202 (London, 1938).

21. *DR*, p. 104

22. *BE*, p. 229

begin in this world, but it cannot reach completion within history. For full realization demands resurrection from the dead, and this can be accomplished only eschatologically. That the kingdom of God *can* in fact be fully realized is a matter of faith. True, Berdyaev is inclined to appeal to belief in the supreme value of personality. But one's ideas of what is desirable, of what one would like to happen, might be frustrated. The confidence that they will not be frustrated is a matter of religious faith. Berdyaev's vision of history is a fruit of his personalism and his Christian faith combined. He had experienced the attraction of the Marxist view of history, but he was convinced that it was incompatible with genuine humanism, with what he understood by personalism.

As Berdyaev insisted that God 'acts only in freedom, only through the freedom of man',[23] it seems to follow that in this view it is possible for human beings to delay or hold up, perhaps indefinitely, realization of the goal of history. This conclusion, however, does not seem to have bothered Berdyaev. For he admitted that just as an individual man can hold up realization of the kingdom of God in himself, so can human beings in general hold up the creation of a new world. Spiritual regeneration does not take place unless a human being cooperates freely with the divine action. It is only when human beings do what they are called to do that what is described as the second coming of Christ can take place. Yet Berdyaev seems to have been confident that at the end of historical time the kingdom of God would be fully realized through the divine power. He did not accept the traditional doctrine of hell, which he regarded as a monstrous idea. Presumably therefore it was for him a matter of religious faith that eventually all human beings without exception would eventually cooperate with the regenerating activity of God.

IV

As Berdyaev laid so much emphasis on the person as a free and creative agent, it is only to be expected that he would be an enemy of collectivism, which he saw as a kind of social monism. On occasion he

23. *SF*, p. 263

carried this enmity to the point of claiming that 'the image of the state will be shown in the final end to be the image of the beast which issues out of the abyss',[24] on the ground that the state has an inbuilt evil will to power and the enslavement of human beings. It is prone, he maintained, to treat human beings simply as means to its own ends, thus manifesting its 'dark and demoniac power'.[25] Father Bulgakov too sometimes used such language, likening the state to the blaspheming beast of the Apocalypse, a beast which he described as untameable, with the result that between it and the Church there could be no real peace.[26]

Given such an unflattering idea of the state, one would hardly expect Berdyaev to attribute to it a positive role in promoting worthwhile social reform. As we noted above[27] however, he does do so, even if perhaps somewhat grudgingly. He aptly remarked, as against the Marxists, that 'there are no good classes, there are only good people'.[28] And he would doubtless be prepared to make a similar remark in regard to states. At the same time he was convinced that the state is a necessary institution in human life, having the function of creating the conditions in which citizens can lead decent human lives and develop their several talents or gifts. In other words Berdyaev saw clearly enough that, in regard to the regulation of material conditions of life, the state must have extensive powers if the individual's freedom to lead a fully human life is to be real and not purely formal. But he also saw that there is a natural tendency on the part of the state to extend its powers as far as it can, and that there is the real danger of the state authorities using human beings as instruments or means to further what are alleged to be the overriding interests of the state.

After his expulsion from his homeland Berdyaev became widely known as a sharp critic and determined foe of collectivism and totalitarianism. The collectivist, he believed, had got his values wrong.

24. *BE*, p. 221

25. *Solitude and Society*, p. 177

26. See, for example, *The Wisdom of God. A Brief Summary of Sophiology*, p. 214 (New York and London, 1937). This work will be referred to in notes as *WG*.

27. Ch. 2, pp. 39–40

28. *DR*, p. 179

Instead of regarding personality as the supreme value, he valued above all things the class or the nation or the state or (Berdyaev would certainly wish to add) the Church. But in capitalism too, according to Berdyaev, there was a distortion of values. As against collectivist socialism on the one hand and capitalism, with its worship of material values, on the other he advocated what he described as personalist socialism, the social expression of seeing in human personality the supreme value. As already noted, the content of personalist socialism was left vague. But Berdyaev might reply to such an objection that, though the philosopher can properly argue in favour of certain value-judgments and draw attention to their general implications, it is not his job to elaborate detailed economic policies or programmes of social-political reform. In any case Berdyaev was certainly not an enemy of all social-political change. He said of himself that, he had never been 'a philosopher of the academic type',[29] and that, with him, 'the desire to know the world has always been accompanied by the desire to alter it'.[30] He would add, of course, that the world cannot be altered for the better unless human beings alter themselves for the better. A genuine respect for human personality would prevent state manipulation of human beings on the one hand and on the other, indifference to want, exploitation and lack of opportunity for personal development.

V

As we have been discussing Berdyaev's ideas of human history, it may be appropriate to refer to his statement that 'a purely objective history would be incomprehensible'.[31] What Berdyaev seems to have in mind, at any rate in part, is that there cannot be historical knowledge without recreation of the past by a subject; that the subject cannot do this without some degree of empathy, of feeling his way into the past and grasping it from within; and that this process results in a fusion of objectivity and subjectivity. The process is possible, according to

29. *Ibid.*, p. 7
30. *Ibid.*
31. *MH*, p. 22

Berdyaev, because each human being is a microcosm of the past, containing in himself or herself 'all the historical epochs of the past which have not been entirely covered over by the subsequent strata of time and of more recent historical life'.[32] When, for example, the historian tries to understand and reconstruct the life of ancient Greece, it is because he is himself the product of the past that he can confer meaning on the objective data to which he refers. In Platonic language, the historian's reconstruction of the past involves a process of 'remembrance'.

When reading Berdyaev, one is not infrequently left wondering precisely how this or that statement should be understood. The question to what extent historiography can be objective provides a familiar topic for critical philosophy of history. One could not reasonably object to Berdyaev discussing the matter. Further, it hardly needs saying that there could be no historiography without reconstruction of the past by a subject. And though any sensible person wants to be able to distinguish between the historical and the fictional, some degree of 'subjectivity' is inevitable. For example, evidence has to be interpreted for it to count as evidence of something. Historiography without some admixture, so to speak, of subjectivity would be impossible. If this were all that Berdyaev meant by claiming that a purely objective history would be incomprehensible, it would be difficult to see how anyone could reasonably object. It is another matter, however, to assert that each human being contains all past historical epochs within himself or herself, and that one can discover in oneself the deep strata of the Hellenic world and the essentials of Greek history. The assertion is, on the face of it, a startling one. It may, of course, be possible to give it a meaning which would make it seem obviously true, but Berdyaev's treatment of the matter is likely to leave the attentive reader wondering how to interpret what has been said. Berdyaev was quite right when he said in his autobiography that he was not an academic philosopher. He was not cut out for painstaking inquiries and analyses in the field of critical philosophy of history. He obviously believed that there were more important things for him to do, that he was a man with a vision and a message and that it was his job to impart them while he had the

32. *Ibid.*, p. 23

opportunity to do so. His speculative philosophy of history was not neutral analysis from an outside standpoint but committed philosophy, intended to form a background for and a spur to creative action in the world.

VI

The idea of the kingdom of God as the goal or end of human history was not, of course, peculiar to Berdyaev, it was shared by other Russian religious thinkers who were expelled from the Soviet Union in 1922. It was rooted in their common Christian faith, and it could obviously coexist with rather different philosophical lines of thought. Thus whereas Berdyaev, though he admired Solovyev, was far from happy with talk about the Absolute and total-unity, Frank and Karsavin stood considerably closer to Solovyev in their metaphysics. As for N.O. Lossky, while he too saw the goal of creation as realization of the kingdom of God, the society of those who have come to share in the divine life through the mediation of the God-man, he laid stress on the idea of free 'substantival agents', and his metaphysics was inspired more by Leibniz's monadology than by German idealism, though he decisively rejected Leibniz's theory of 'windowless' monads.

In 1923 Lev Platonovich Karsavin published his work *The Philosophy of History* at Berlin. Among the themes which he discussed was the nature of causality as exemplified in the relations between the life of a people and its natural environment as well as between different nations or peoples. Another theme was the role of the concept of novelty in historical thinking and research. As, however, one would expect in the case of a thinker who stood close to Solovyev in the emphasis which he laid on the idea of total-unity, Karsavin developed these lines of thought within the framework of a metaphysics which represented history as a unified process and as part of the cosmic process of the self-manifestation of the Absolute. It should be added, however, that the whole cosmic process was interpreted in the light of belief in the Incarnation. Further, Karsavin, like Solovyev before him, expounded the idea of cooperation between Church and state in seeking to promote, in appropriate ways, approximation to realization of the goal of history. In other words, Karsavin's philosophy of history was clearly part of a general Christian world-view, a fact which he made no attempt to conceal.

According to Berdyaev, the theme of the end or goal of history was one of those which were specifically Russian. One might feel inclined to object that there is nothing specifically Russian in the theme. If it is assumed that the world was created by a personal God, the theme is almost bound to arise, even if the problem is then dismissed as insoluble. Berdyaev, however, maintained that 'our creative philosophical thought' had manifested 'a yearning for the kingdom of God, together with a sense of the impossibility of reconciling oneself to this world'.[33] By the phrase 'our creative philosophical thought' Berdyaev presumably meant what he regarded as creative development of a native Russian tradition of religiously oriented thought, as distinct from philosophical movements and ideas coming in from the West and at variance with the native Russian spirit. In support of his point of view one might appeal to the idea of the goal of history which was common to Solovyev and his spiritual heirs, on the ground that they were trying to fulfil the demand made by Kireevsky and Khomyakov for the development of Russian philosophical thought issuing from religious faith and presenting a Christian world-view. This line of thought would hardly dispose of the objection that the theme of the goal of history was a prominent feature of Marxism, and that Marxism was an importation from western Europe and certainly not a Russian creation. But Berdyaev might retort that the messianic aspect of Marxism was stressed much more in Russia than by Karl Marx himself, and that this tends to confirm the thesis that the theme of the goal of history was a characteristic of Russian philosophical thought. True, Marxism was atheistic and did not look forward to realization of the kingdom of God, but its idea of a universal and truly human society was a secularized version of this concept.

Concern with ultimate problems, Berdyaev asserted, was shown more by 'the great literary figures of Russia'[34] than by her professional philosophers. And it is obviously true that the theme of the goal of history appears in the writings of both Dostoevsky and Tolstoy. But it is

33. *BE*, p. 35

34. *Ibid.*

reasonable to associate the theme much more with Judaeo-Christian beliefs than with any specifically Russian origins. After all, Solovyev and his spiritual heirs were contributing to the development of a Christian world-view, and that the Christian thinker cannot be indifferent to human history is a commonplace. In so far as Marxism is seen as including a messianic element, it too stemmed from Judaeo-Christian origins. With the Russian religious thinkers there was a strong tendency to regard religious themes as inspired by a native Russian tradition of thought and non-religious themes as importations from western Europe. This idea may show an admirable love of Russia, but it can be exaggerated.

Chapter 4

The human being: the concept of Godmanhood

According to Berdyaev, creative philosophical thought in Russia was principally concerned with problems in philosophy of history, philosophy of religion and moral philosophy. He further maintained that certain themes were 'specifically Russian'.[1] Among other examples he mentioned the subject of Godmanhood, which had been developed by Solovyev and by the Russian religious philosophers of the beginning of the twentieth century. Berdyaev was doubtless thinking of writers such as Prince Sergey Trubetskoy (1862–1905), Rector of the University of Moscow, and his brother, Prince Evgeny Trubetskoy (1863–1920), who published a work in which he examined Solovyev's thought and tried to bring it more into line with what he believed to be the requirements of Orthodoxy.

The objection may be raised that the theme of Godmanhood was based on the New Testament and on the writings of the Fathers of the Church, and that there was nothing specifically Russian about it. To see the connection with the New Testament, we have only to read such passages as the first chapter of *Ephesians* or the first two chapters of *Colossians*, not to speak of the eighth chapter of *Romans*, to which Solovyev liked to refer. As for the patristic writings, we find in them the doctrine, already presented in the first chapter of St Peter's second Epistle, that human beings are called to participate in the divine life.

When, however, Berdyaev referred to the theme of Godmanhood as being specifically Russian, he obviously did not intend to deny its scriptural basis, nor its essential connection with the Christian doctrine of the Incarnation. Nor need we interpret him as claiming that the theme was never treated by a non-Russian thinker; for example,

1. *BE*, p. 35

Schelling introduced the theme in his philosophy of mythology and revelation. What Berdyaev meant was that the subject was explicitly developed by Russian philosophers, in particular by Solovyev and his spiritual heirs, rather than by western thinkers.

There is a very good reason, it may be said, for this situation. While the subject of Godmanhood, as expressing reflection on the doctrine of the Incarnation and its implications, certainly has a role to play in Christian theology, it is not an appropriate topic for the philosopher, not at any rate if we presuppose the distinction between philosophy and Christian theology which has emerged in western thought and is largely taken for granted in the West. A writer may, of course, employ some philosophical ideas and techniques in clarifying and developing the idea of Godmanhood, but this does not alter the fact that they are being used within and in the service of Christian theological thought. In so far as Berdyaev is justified in claiming that the theme of Godmanhood is characteristic of Russian creative philosophy, it is because his idea of what constitutes creative philosophical thought is not limited by any sharp division between specifically theological and specifically philosophical topics.

In connection with this line of thought we can profitably recall a remark made by N.O. Lossky, namely that 'the classical Thomistic distinction between rational and revealed truth was utterly foreign to Solovyev'.[2] To say this of all Solovyev's spiritual heirs might be putting the matter rather too strongly, but Lossky's remark is clearly true of Solovyev himself. Solovyev had a broad concept of revelation, one which covered the whole history of religion and religious thought. For instance, the religiously oriented philosophy of Plotinus represented for him a stage in the unfolding of revealed truth. As for the concept of Godmanhood, it certainly had its basis in the New Testament, but it needed to be understood, developed and applied in the light of subsequent thought. This process of thinking or systematic reflection, inspired by Christian faith, was precisely the sort of 'philosophizing' for which, as we have already seen, Russian religious thinkers such as Kireevsky and Khomyakov believed that there was a crying need. For Solovyev and his successors the subject of Godmanhood had its place in the development of a general Christian world-view which, in western

2. *A Solovyev Anthology*, arranged by S.L. Frank, translated by N. Duddington, p. 15 (London, 1950). Quoted from Frank's Introduction.

terms, would be neither exclusively philosophical nor exclusively theological. Philosophical anthropology was for them an essential feature of philosophy, but they were convinced that there could be no adequate philosophy of the human being, the human person, if the theme of Godmanhood were excluded.

A Thomist might be inclined to comment that, although it is true that there can be no adequate concept of the human person if the person's relationship to God through Christ is excluded, this simply means that philosophy alone cannot provide us with an adequate understanding of the human being, and that, to supplement philosophical truth, we have to turn to divine revelation and to theological reflection on revealed truth. However this may be, Solovyev at any rate did not think in this sort of way. As Lossky rightly said, the classical Thomist distinction between philosophy and Christian theology was foreign to his mind. And it was foreign to his mind because, as I remarked, he had a broad concept of revelation and did not make any rigid distinction between revealed and non-revealed truth. Referring to a thirteenth-century Russian writer, George P. Fedotov notes how the author in question simply includes the Incarnation and Resurrection of Christ in a chain of historical facts. For Fedotov this implies that, in the eyes of the writer, the whole of history, without any distinction between 'sacred' and 'profane', has 'a religious meaning'.[3] Up to a point at any rate we can see this kind of attitude as manifesting itself at a much later date in the religiously oriented philosophy which was looked forward to by Kireevsky and Khomyakov and which Solovyev and his spiritual heirs endeavoured to develop. Given their approach and general programme, their reflection on the human person in the light of Christian belief was natural enough and only what one might expect.

II

If someone who has heard that Solovyev expounded a theory of Godmanhood, and who wishes to become acquainted with it, turns for enlightenment to the philosopher's *Lectures on Godmanhood*, he or she may very well experience a feeling of perplexity or perhaps disappointment. For after having learned a good deal about Solovyev's

3. *The Russian Religious Mind*, by George P. Fedotov, vol. I, p. 383 (Cambridge, Mass., 1946).

views on the nature and history of religion, readers find themselves confronted by a philosophical deduction of the triune nature of the Absolute or God, followed by a metaphysics of creation. It is only later on that Solovyev comes to the subject of Godmanhood. Even then relatively little is said about the God-man in the sense of Christ as depicted in the Gospels. It is Christ's cosmic role and his function as head of a universal divine-human organism, developing through history, which is stressed.

To say this is obviously equivalent to asserting that in Solovyev's thought the theory of Godmanhood forms an integral part of a general interpretation of reality and human history. Starting with the concept of the ultimate reality, the One, Solovyev argues that the One must differentiate itself internally (and eternally) into three hypostases which are none the less one Absolute, one God, in virtue of each having the same substance. In effect Solovyev undertakes a logical deduction of the Christian doctrine of the Trinity. Trying to prove the truth of this doctrine by *a priori* metaphysical arguments, he pursues a line of thought which owes much to Hellenistic thought and to German idealism. By this deduction of the triune nature of the ultimate reality Solovyev finds a basis in the Absolute itself for the emergence of plurality, first of an ideal world of essence or ideas and then in what we ordinarily think of as creation. For Solovyev, it pertains to the nature of God as love to express himself objectively through creation, in a plurality which at the same time remains comprised within the divine total-unity. Considered in this light, creation is not only necessary but also good. To be sure, the emergence of individual entities has involved the appearance of egoism, of self-assertion on the part of the indiviual being to the extent of its acting as though it were the only pebble on the beach, as though it aspired to be the All. Looked at from this point of view, creation can be described as a Fall. It expresses a loss of or a falling away from unity, a fragmentation. As, however, nothing can possibly exist apart from or outside the Absolute, entirely outside the total-unity, the loss cannot be complete. There thus remains the possibility of a return to unity. Indeed, it is not simply a question of mere possibility. For, according to Solovyev, there is in the world a tendency or striving (described as the world-soul) towards the overcoming of fragmentation, disharmony and strife, a striving which expresses itself in the ascending levels of evolution, until in the human being the

world-soul is 'united with the divine Logos in consciousness'.[4] That is
to say, in the human being, through illumination by the divine Logos or
Word, the inarticulate striving after the restoration of unity, after union
with God, becomes conscious of itself.

This process of illumination or revelation is not completed all at
once. It is a gradual process, as can be seen by reflecting on the history
of religion, which Solovyev conceives as a series of successive stages of
God's self-revelation, from primitive religions up to Christianity. The
history of religion is represented as the history of the development of
the religious consciousness, and in Christianity all previous phases of
the religious consciousness are subsumed and united, becoming 'parts
of it'.[5] The perfect religion, Solovyev insists, is 'not that which is equally
contained in all',[6] a religious least common multiple; it is 'that which
contains all of them in itself and possesses all'.[7] This ideal, he
maintains, is realized in the Christian religion.

Solovyev did not, of course, claim that the return to unity, to the
One, could be accomplished simply by a process of mental illumination,
by assenting to certain truths. If selfishness and enmity in human life
were to be overcome, an inner transformation or regeneration of the
soul was required. This transformation was conceived by Solovyev as
taking the form of incorporation with Christ. The Incarnation was
represented as 'a more perfect theophany in a series of other, imperfect,
preparatory' theophanies.[8] It was seen by Solovyev as required in order
that the return to God by a fallen world could take place. Christ was
regarded as the active principle of the process of return, as the head of a
divine-human organism, 'regenerated, spiritual humanity'.[9] This organism, the mystical body of Christ, was at first only potentially universal,
but Solovyev believed that this potentiality would be progressively
actualized, until eventually it comprised the whole of humanity. In

---

4. *Lectures on Godmanhood*, with an introduction by Peter P. Zouboff, p. 198
   (New York, 1944). From Lecture X. This translation will be referred to in notes as
   LG.

5. *Ibid.*, p. 165. From Lecture VII.

6. *Ibid.*, p. 110. From Lecture III.

7. *Ibid.*

8. *Ibid.*, p. 212. From Lectures XI and XII, which are printed as one.

9. *Ibid.*, p. 210

some way the return to unity would include the physical world; there would be a transfiguration of the cosmos. But Solovyev was principally concerned, of course, with the return of mankind, with the development of the Church considered as the mystical body of Christ, as the prolongation, so to speak, of the Incarnation of the Logos in Jesus of Nazareth.

Some explanatory notes may be appropriate. In the first place, even if Berdyaev was justified in seeing in Solovyev's thought a tendency to monism, Solovyev did not in fact conceive the return of the Many to the One as involving the obliteration of the former, a swallowing up of the Many by an all-devouring One. The Incarnation of the Logos did not mean obliteration of the humanity of Jesus. Analogously, participation by human beings in Godmanhood should not be conceived as involving the disappearance of the distinctions between persons or between them and God. What is overcome is not personality as such but rather alienation from God and from other human beings. The person who participates in Godmanhood is still human.

A second explanatory note. As we have seen, Solovyev envisaged the growth of a divine-human organism, identified with the Church in the sense of the mystical body of Christ. In the *Lectures on Godmanhood* he spoke in a manner which reminds us of Slavophile writers such as Kireevsky. That is to say, he depicted the Eastern Church as having preserved 'the truth of Christ',[10] even if it had not expressed this truth externally in the form of a genuinely Christian culture. By way of contrast to the Eastern Church's fidelity to the truth of Christ, the Roman Catholic Church was represented as having succumbed to the desire for power and to the temptation to employ coercion as a means of attaining a good end. As for Protestantism, it was said to pass naturally into rationalism.[11] If, however, we turn to *Russia and the Universal Church*, which Solovyev wrote in French and published at Paris in 1889, we find a very different attitude. We are told, for example, that the Byzantine government always supported heresy, and that the Russian Orthodox Church is 'totally subservient to the secular power and destitute of all inner vitality'.[12] By this time Solovyev had

10. *Ibid.*, p. 224

11. *Ibid.*, 221

12. *Russia and the Universal Church*, p. 51.

discarded Slavophile exaltation of Holy Mother Russia at the expense
of the West and instead stressed the positive role of Catholics in the
historical development of Christianity. In view, however, of the clash
between these two positions it is important to understand that, when
Solovyev talks about Christ as the spiritual centre of a universal
organism and describes this organism as the Church, the mystical body
of Christ, what he has in mind is not this or that particular Church but
the whole community of those who are spiritually united to Christ and
participate in Godmanhood. At no time was he so narrow-minded as to
claim that participation in Godmanhood is restricted to members of
some particular Christian Church.

In the third place, though Solovyev certainly regarded his world-view
as expressing knowledge, theoretical knowledge, this knowledge was
conceived as having a practical function, as serving as an 'educative and
directive force in life'.[13] Similarly, the theory of Godmanhood was
conceived as oriented to practice or action. We can say that the
practical function of the idea of Godmanhood was to stimulate man's
free subjection of his will to the divine will, in union with Christ's
subjection of his human will to the will of the Father. But this free union
of one's own will with that of God was seen by Solovyev as inseparable
from incorporation in the divine-human organism which grows in time
until its potential universality is realized. The concept of Godmanhood
was thus a social concept, in the sense that it had a social aspect which
was an essential feature of it. It should awaken and stimulate a practical
interest in the transformation of society, a transformation affecting not
only interior attitudes but also social and economic conditions.

III

It is hardly necessary to say that the idea of Godmanhood, if understood as meaning that human beings are called to union with God
through the mediation of Christ, the God-man in the fullest sense of the
term, was common to all of Solovyev's Christian successors. Thus S.L.
Frank referred to 'the very essence of Christianity as (being) the religion

13. *SS*, I, p. 291. From *Philosophical Principles*, 2.

of Godmanhood',[14] and though Berdyaev did not make frequent use of the word 'Godmanhood', he regarded the doctrine as one of the characteristic features of Russian religious thought. True, he had some reservations in regard to Solovyev's exposition of the theory, but he looked on the basic idea as an essential element of a Christian philosophy of the human person. Indeed, an association between the idea of Godmanhood and the idea of humanism was a common feature of the treatments of the first idea by Solovyev's spiritual heirs.

Though the word 'humanism' certainly need not be understood as implying either indifference or hostility to religion, it has in fact been sometimes taken as involving the view either that religion is not required for the full development of the personality or that it is positively harmful to the human being, stunting intellectual growth and making it impossible to see the world and human history as they really are. As against humanism in this sense Solovyev's successors insisted that any adequate version of it demands recognition of the human being's relationship to God, to transcendent reality. It was their conviction that the human being cannot attain his or her full stature, unless the potentiality of union with God through Christ, the God-man *par excellence*, is actualized. There is more in man than non-religious humanism allows.

By way of exemplifying and enlarging upon these observations I wish to say something about particular ways in which one or two of Solovyev's successors treated the relationship between humanism and the idea of Godmanhood. To describe these I select Frank and Berdyaev. Though both thinkers criticized non-religious humanism as expounding inadequate and distorted ideas of the human being, there are some differences in emphasis between their respective treatments of the subject.

IV

While Frank did not, of course, deny that through his psycho-physical nature man belongs to the objective world, the world of the empirical

14. *Reality and Man. An Essay in the Metaphysics of Human Nature*, translated by N. Duddington, p. 122 (London, 1965). This work will be referred to in notes as *RM*.

sciences—the world, as Frank put it, of fact—he argued that there are aspects of man which indicate that, in spite of being a member of the world of fact, of science, man can also transcend this world. One such feature of the human being is the ability to evaluate facts, to sit in judgment on them. In exercising this ability the human being, according to Frank, transcends the world of fact. Further, this is possible because the human being is essentially related to transcendent reality. Thus Frank asserts that 'man's relation to, or connection with God is the determining characteristic of man's very being'.[15] It is true that man distinguishes himself from God as a transcendent reality 'out there'. That is to say, this attitude is clearly a feature of the ordinary religious consciousness. But God is not in actual fact 'out there'; he penetrates man's being as its source and centre. Frank can thus say that his main aim in writing his book *Reality and Man* was 'to affirm the indissoluble connection between the idea of God and the idea of man, i.e. to justify the conception of 'Godmanhood' in which I find the central meaning of the Christian faith'.[16] In this case it obviously follows that any form of humanism which is indifferent or hostile to religion in general and Christianity in particular is inevitably inadequate. 'That which makes man human—the principle of *humanity* in man— is his Godmanhood'.[17]

Frank warns his readers that it is a mistake to interpret him as being concerned simply with reaffirming the old distinction between soul and body or even between man as a psycho-physical organism on the one hand and as spirit on the other. For the distinction which he is intent on making can be found even within what has been described as the soul or as the self. For example, the self in the sense of the pure ego, the epistemological subject, is a point without content and cannot be reasonably identified with the self in its inmost reality. According to Frank, we should make a distinction between the self-conscious subject and agent on the one hand and the inmost depth of the self on the other, awareness of which is akin to mystical experience. It does not follow, however, that the human being is to be conceived as consisting of two heterogeneous entities. The human being 'is not simply dual, but is a

15. *Ibid.*, p. 112

16. *Ibid.*, p. xiii

17. *Ibid.*, p. 112

bi-unity'.[18] It is a question not of two juxtaposed entities but of 'two different levels or layers in the human spirit itself'.[19]

The general idea can possibly be made clearer in this way. To the self-conscious human subject God necessarily appears as a transcendent Thou, beyond or external to the self. To the self-conscious subject God cannot appear except as a correlative object, as something over against the self. Indeed, the I-Thou relationship 'is the essence of the purely religious attitude as such'.[20] Though, however, Frank does not intend to deny the divine transcendence, he none the less claims that God 'constitutes man's inmost being'.[21] In his view, if God and the human being are conceived as 'absolutely heterogeneous entities logically prior to the relation between them',[22] the two concepts can then be described as 'unrealizable abstractions'.[23] The concepts cease to be pure abstractions and acquire positive meaning, we are told, only when they are seen as referring to 'indivisible aspects of Godmanhood as the truly primary principle'.[24]

It is hardly necessary to say that if Frank is right in claiming that God constitutes the inmost reality of the human being and that the distinct concepts of God and man are formed by abstraction from 'Godmanhood', he is fully justified in claiming that non-religious humanism cannot furnish us with any adequate conception of the human being. But are the premises acceptable? Apart from any other line of objection, Frank sees that his idea of Godmanhood is likely to prompt a good many Christian readers to ask whether the unique position of Christ as God-man has not been overlooked or even implicitly denied. After all, do not Christians believe that any participation in the divine life, any elevation to the status of children of God, depends on the mediation of Jesus Christ, who is Son of the Father in a unique sense? If God

18. *Ibid.*, p. 34

19. *Ibid.*, p. 141

20. *Ibid.*, p.113

21. *Ibid.*, p. 139

22. *Ibid.*

23. *Ibid.*

24. *Ibid.*

constitutes the inmost reality of every human being without exception, the idea of the unique position and role of Christ must surely disappear. Like Solovyev before him, Frank expounded a metaphysics of total-unity, God being conceived as the all-embracing and all-pervading reality, outside of which there is not and cannot be anything. In the light of this metaphysics does he not universalize a relationship which Christians traditionally believe to have been exemplified uniquely in Christ?

As a devout Christian Frank is quite ready to assert that there is an 'immeasurable difference between the average man and the God-man Jesus Christ'.[25] At the same time he claims that the doctrine that God became *man* (rather than any kind of non-human being, that is to say) clearly 'bears testimony to an affinity between God and man'.[26] For it to be possible for the human being to participate in the divine life, to be united with God, there must be in the human being from the start a divine element which makes a man or woman a potential sharer in the divine life. If God became man in order that man might become God, there must be something in man which makes that elevation possible. If we are prepared to admit this, Frank argues, and only if we are so prepared, the perfect Incarnation in Christ 'loses its arbitrary character and fits in with the general meaning of human life and nature. Vladimir Solovyev has shown this most convincingly'.[27]

On the one hand Frank allows that there are ways in which 'man is obviously different from God'.[28] For example, the human being, if considered precisely as a psycho-physical organism, is obviously different from God as conceived by Christians, Jews and Moslems. On the other hand, however, Frank claims that man and God are 'unthinkable apart from each other'.[29] In support of this claim he refers to the testimony of mystics such as Angelus Silesius and, in Islam, Mansur al-Hallāj, who expressed what they were convinced was a genuine

25. *Ibid.*, p. 140

26. *Ibid.*, p. 141

27. *Ibid.*

28. *Ibid.*, p. 135

29. *Ibid.*, p. 134

consciousness of the divine presence in the depths of their souls. But statements made by some mystics to express this consciousness led to accusations of blasphemy, on the ground that they had laid claim to identity with God. This was notably the case with Al-Hallāj, who was put to death.[30] It is at any rate arguable that if speech is found necessary in preference to silence, poetry is perhaps the best medium for conveying some notion of mystical experience of oneness with God, and that the relevant relationship cannot be described with the clarity and precision which can be reasonably expected of a philosopher. Thus Frank finds himself impelled to make such cryptic statements as 'I am aware of Him as the inner basis of my being precisely in so far as He is different from me'.[31]

The point which I am trying to make is really this. Frank certainly developed and expounded a systematic metaphysics, a metaphysics in which N.O. Lossky discerned 'too great an approximation between God and the world'.[32] But the influence of mysticism, or at any rate of reflection on mysticism, on his thought should not be lost to view. Already in his early work *The Object of Knowledge* (1915) he had spoken of the ultimate, all-embracing unity as 'metalogical', in the sense that it transcends all oppositions and contradictions and cannot be given adequate conceptual expression. And the title of a later work, *The Unfathomable* (1939) may suggest that in regard to the nature of the ultimate reality a policy of silence might well be observed. For if 'the fathomable', identified with the world of objects, can be grasped conceptually whereas the Unfathomable is said to be unobjectifiable and to elude conceptualization, how can we be justified in trying to speak about it? Will not our language inevitably fail to achieve its aim? In *Reality and Man*, the work to which I have been referring, Frank replies to this sort of objection or query by arguing that 'our experience is wider than our thought'[33], and that even when what we experience eludes conceptualization, we are not necessarily doomed to remain

---

30. Some scholars have maintained that the real reasons for Al-Hallàj's execution were of a political nature.

31. *RM*, p. 114

32. *History of Russian Philosophy*, p. 283 (London, 1952).

33. *RM*, p. 41

dumb, as though our experience were 'utterly inaccessible to thought'.[34] Art, he maintains, bears witness to the contrary. And poetry in particular is 'a mysterious way of expressing things that cannot be put in an abstract logical form'.[35] If it is objected that philosophy and poetry are not the same thing, Frank answers that the difference 'is not absolute, but relative'[36]. There can be a combination of concepts which, taken together, suggest the nature of reality to the mind and, in this limited sense, can be said to describe it. When, therefore, in *Reality and Man* Frank writes about the relationship between God and the world and, in particular, between the human being and God, he looks on himself as using suggestive language which by its very nature is open to rationalistic objection on one score or another. The language will have meaning for anyone who has enjoyed to some degree the mystical experience of the presence of God in the soul or of the grounding of the human spirit in God. He or she will be able to recognize what is being referred to, in spite of the inadequate and potentially misleading language employed. But in the case of someone who completely lacks the relevant experience what is said about the relationships in question will simply give rise to what might be described as objections of the head. A good deal of what poets say is open to such objections, but the language used can be a means of conveying truth.

However all this may be, it should be added that, while Frank obviously hoped that exposition of the theory of Godmanhood would help his readers to become more aware of their inner relationship to God, he did not wish to encourage a mystical quietism, in the sense of a more or less complete withdrawal from the world of action. He argued that the more man is conscious of himself as being made in the image and likeness of God, and the more he participates in the divine life, so much the more is he conscious of himself as sharing derivatively in the divine creativity. God, according to Frank, 'creates creators ...and grants his creatures a share in his own creativeness'.[37] Participation in Godmanhood should issue in 'theandric' action, creative action which

34. *Ibid.*

35. *Ibid.*

36. *Ibid.*, p. 42

37. *Ibid.*, p. 157

is, so to speak, the joint action of God and the human being. In concrete terms, 'the creation of new and better forms of social life is the natural purpose of man's creative will'.[38]

In view of the emphasis laid by Frank on the relationship between the human being and God and on Christ as God-man in the fullest sense, it is obvious that the last-quoted statement should not be interpreted as expressing any desire for the secularization of religion in general or Christianity in particular. Frank was not suggesting that the Christian ideal of the kingdom of God should be transformed into that of the kingdom of Man to the exclusion of God, a kingdom to be realized in this world or not at all. Social-political activity was for him 'a necessary and legitimate sphere of human creativeness'[39], and he regarded it as the business of the state to create and maintain the most favourable external conditions for the development of the human being's moral and spiritual life. But it is not the job of the state to try to save mankind or to pose as 'supreme master of man's life'.[40] It is God who saves, not the state. The more the state trespasses on 'the sacred and inviolable sphere of personal freedom'[41], the more does it merit Nietzsche's description of it as 'the coldest of all cold monsters'. But though the state is capable of becoming a demonic power, it is none the less a necessary institution, which has the function of creating the most favourable external conditions for the leading of a truly human life, a life, which, for Frank, is one lived in union and free cooperation with God. This means that the genuine Christian should contribute, according to his or her abilities and opportunities, to the creative work of the political society to which he or she belongs. Frank expresses agreement with Henri Bergson in his view that a distinguishing mark of the divine creativity is that God creates creators, creative agents through whom the end or goal of world-creation can be realized. Godmanhood does not mean setting up a barrier against 'the world' and cultivating inaction. For it is in and through human activity that the divine creative activity reveals itself. According to Frank, it is only through a process of

38. *Ibid.*, p. 188

39. *Ibid.*

40. *Ibid.*

41. *Ibid.*, p. 187

mental abstraction that God and the human being can be set over
against one another as completely heterogeneous entities.

V

As both Frank and Berdyaev were Christian believers, fellow members
of the Russian Orthodox Church, one would naturally expect to find a
substantial measure of agreement between them on the subject of
Godmanhood. When Berdyaev states that one of the chief merits of
Solovyev was that 'he tried to give a religious meaning to the experience
of humanism',[42] Frank would obviously have no quarrel with the
statement. Again, Frank would certainly endorse Berdyaev's assertions
that man 'can only be interpreted through his relation to God'[43] and
that the central idea of Christian anthropology is 'that of the God-
man'.[44] Similarly, when Berdyaev claims that 'the doctrine of Godmanhood presupposes commensurability between God and man, the
presence of a divine principle in man',[45] the claim is one which, as we
have noted, was also made by Frank. Further if Frank spoke, as he did,
of human beings as called to share in the divine creativity, we would
expect Berdyaev, who laid so much emphasis on human freedom and
creative initiative, to adopt substantially the same idea. So indeed he
did. He tells us, for example, that 'man, made by God in his own image
and likeness, is also a creator and is called to creative work'.[46] Human
creativity was a theme with which Berdyaev had concerned himself
even before the first world war, the fruit of his reflections being *The
Meaning of the Creative Act* (1916). Looking back at a later date he
remarked that in *The Destiny of Man* (1931) the idea of man as creator
'was better developed but with less passion'.[47] The subject, he adds, is
metaphysical, treating not simply of man's creativity in art or in the

42. *The Russian Idea*, translated by R.M. French, p. 91 (London, 1947).

43. *The Destiny of Man*, translated by N. Duddington, p. 60 (London, 1937). This
    translation will be referred to in notes as *DM*.

44. *Ibid.*, p. 61

45. BE, p. 36

46. DM, p. 163

47. *The Russian Idea*, p. 242

sciences but also, and rather, of 'the continuation by man of the creation of the world'.[48] As we have seen, Frank too conceived the human being as called to participate in the creative activity of God.

The fact that Frank and Berdyaev shared a common Christian faith obviously meant that they were at one in rejecting non-religious humanism, and in claiming that no adequate philosophical anthropology is possible unless the human being's relationship to God is recognized. It does not follow however that no differences can be discerned between their respective conceptions of human nature and activity. Consider, for example, the theme of human creativeness. According to Frank, 'there can be no true creativeness apart from moral earnestness and responsibility' and 'it must be combined with humility'.[49] Berdyaev, however, draws attention to 'a tragic conflict between creativeness and personal perfection ...When a man begins to seek moral perfection ...he may be lost to creative work'.[50] As for humility, Berdyaev describes creativeness and humility as 'conflicting moral tendencies'.[51] True, he does not maintain that creativeness is incompatible with the adoption of any moral ideals whatsoever. What he maintains is that there is an 'ethics of creativeness [which] is different from the ethics of redemption',[52] being concerned not with personal salvation but with the realization of values. For example 'the ethics of creativeness affirms the value of the unique and the individual',[53] a value to which, in Berdyaev's opinion, Christian ethics was for a long time blind. For him, the ethics of creativeness is 'the highest and most mature form of moral consciousness',[54] superior to any ethics which attaches little or no value to creative freedom and originality, to rising above the common herd.

If we are interested in trying to iron out or to diminish what may at

48. *Ibid.*, p. 243

49. *RM*, p. 160

50. *DM*, p. 168

51. *Ibid.*, p. 173

52. *Ibid.*, p. 171

53. *Ibid.*, pp. 171–2

54. *Ibid.*, p. 181

first glance seem to be diametrically opposed and irreconcilable posi-
tons, it is doubtless possible to do so, up to a point that is to say. When
Frank said that there could be no true creativeness apart from moral
earnestness and that it must be accompanied by humility, he was clearly
thinking of 'true creativeness' as participation in God's creative activity,
and he was claiming that one cannot be said to be doing God's work in
the world if one pays no attention to the demands of morality and if one
denies one's dependence on God. Rejection of moral principles pro-
duces criminals, and criminals who attain power and wreck other
people's lives are none the less criminals if they claim to be and like to
be regarded as carrying on 'creative political work'.[55] It hardly needs
saying that Berdyaev would be in substantial agreement with this line of
thought. For him, respect for human freedom and for the individual
person was a basic value. He has no sympathy with the idea of some
leader or dictator trying to mould mankind according to his own ideas
of what human beings should be. When he referred to a conflict
between creative work and the search for moral perfection and between
creativeness and humility, he was thinking, for example, of the way in
which the pursuit of an ascetic ideal of moral perfection and selflessness
tended to lead people to renounce the exercise and development of
artistic and literary talents as conducive to pride and as smacking of
'worldliness'. As a firm believer that God bestows talents for use and
development (and perhaps, to some extent, as a Russian aristocrat), he
was convinced that the world would be a much poorer place if the
ascetic ideal prevailed over the 'ethics of creativeness'. But he certainly
did not mean to imply that all moral ideals should be thrown out of the
window. He did not need to be told that Godmanhood could not be
realized through, for example, hatred and cruelty towards other human
beings.

Though the differences between Frank and Berdyaev can be exaggerated, or over-emphasized, they are real enough. Frank, like Solovyev
before him, aimed at synthesis and harmonization. For example,
though he explicitly admitted that in its own domain 'artistic creativeness knows no criteria except artistic perfection',[56] he went on to claim

55. *RM*, p. 189
56. *Ibid.*, p. 160

that, in life as a whole, creativeness should be subject to the principles of, as he put it, holiness. He was interested in human life as a whole, in the sense that, while recognizing actual or potential conflicts between distinguishable activities or forms of life, he wished to show how these different activities could together form a harmonious whole. But whereas Frank, a philosopher of total-unity, was naturally interested in synthesis, Berdyaev, influenced strongly by both Dostoevsky and Nietzsche, liked to underline sharp contrasts. Though he paid tribute to Solovyev as a Christian humanist and as 'the most outstanding philosopher of the nineteenth century',[57] he was far from sharing Solovyev's enthusiasm for synthesis. 'In him [Solovyev] there were no tragic conflicts and yawning gulfs, such as are disclosed in Dostoevsky'.[58] When we are told that the ethics of creativeness 'is not the social morality of the herd',[59] the name of Nietzsche immediately comes to mind. Berdyaev does not try to make out that conventional morality, and what he calls the ethics of creativeness, are really complementary and fit together in a harmonious ethical whole; on the contrary, he draws attention to the element of opposition or conflict. He showed scant sympathy with philosophical systems as such. He saw them as trying to play down or gloss over the oppositions and conflicts which are an obvious feature of human life. But while he certainly sympathized with Nietzsche's attitude to the way in which 'the herd' endeavours to pull down the creative spirits to its own level, he was none the less convinced that all human beings have the potentiality of Godmanhood, and that Immanuel Kant was perfectly justified in claiming that the human person should never be treated as a mere means. It was in the name of a profoundly religious humanism that he attacked the ideology expounded by the new rulers of his native land.

VI

With the Russian religious philosophers the concept of Godmanhood was inseparably linked with belief in the Incarnation and was clearly

57. *The Russian Idea*, p. 166

58. *Ibid.*, p. 92

59. *DM*, p. 182

derived from the Christian religion. It was then used in speculative philosophy of history to give meaning to the historical process. Does it follow that the Russian thinkers looked on universal realization of Godmanhood as inevitable, as a goal which will be attained without fail? To ask this is the same as asking whether, for the thinkers in question, eventual realization of the kingdom of God is inevitable and can be predicted with certainty. It may seem perhaps that the idea of the kingdom of God is a social idea or has a social bearing, whereas the concept of Godmanhood relates simply to the individual human being's participation in the divine life. We have to remember, however, that, for Solovyev, Godmanhood was attainable only in and through membership of a divine-human organism. And though talk about a social organism was, for Berdyaev, rather like the proverbial red rag to a bull, he none the less insisted that realization of Godmanhood involved not only the regeneration of individuals but also the transfiguration of society.

Given Berdyaev's assertion that the concept of freedom, and not that of being, lay at the basis of his philosophical thought, it was only to be expected that he would find fault with Solovyev for having written as though the full realization of Godmanhood were 'a necessary determined process of evolution'.[60] It is natural that he should have insisted that realization of the kingdom of God depends not only on divine action but also on the human being's exercise of his or her freedom. If human freedom is taken seriously, does it not follow that, just as the individual can hinder the realization of Godmanhood within himself or herself, so is it possible for mankind in general to stand in the way of realization of the kingdom of God?

Turning to Frank, we might expect that his metaphysics of total-unity and his idea of the world, including human history, as a divine theophany would lead him to look on history as a progressive advance towards the inevitable realization of an ideal goal, predetermined by the nature of the One. In fact, however, we find him expressing a markedly different point of view. Referring to that 'comfortably optimistic faith in the certainty of a continuous moral and intellectual progress, in the easy possibility of realizing on earth the kingdom of reason, justice and

60. *The Russian Idea*, p. 173

goodness', he describes it as 'blind and, indeed, ridiculous ...for it is contrary to all historical experience'.[61] He disclaims any intention of trying to provide 'a metaphysical justification of the idea of continuous pre-established progress'.[62] Indeed, Frank goes on to say that we have no guarantee whatever that the cultural level already attained by mankind will be preserved in the future. For the matter of that we do not know that 'our small planet is the foreordained centre of the world's spiritual history'.[63] For all we know, the process begun on our planet may continue and end elsewhere.

When Frank dismisses the idea of inevitable progress in history, he is thinking in the first place of theories asserting the inevitable progressive realization of a terrestrial paradise, a kingdom of Man on earth. At the same time his insistence that any such theory runs counter to historical experience obviously applies to any claim that human history manifests a continuous process of advance, even if full realization of the envisaged goal is conceived as reserved for the next world. To be sure, Frank maintains that we can be certain of 'God's final victory'[64] which, he tells us (in a manner recalling Solovyev's expectations in his later years), is 'likely to be sudden and unexpected, following the apparent defeat of the Divine powers by the unbridled forces of evil and chaos'.[65] But this confidence in the eschatological triumph of light over darkness, good over evil, was a matter of Christian faith, a faith which the devout Christian preserves in spite of all that 'historical experience' may suggest.

This Christian faith was shared by Berdyaev. He does indeed say that history has a meaning because of the Incarnation and because 'it is moving towards the realm of Godmanhood'.[66] But history has this meaning when it is seen with the eyes of faith; it is not a matter of historical laws which can be discerned by the philosopher of history.

61. *RM*, p. 126

62. *Ibid.*, p. 222

63. *Ibid.*

64. *Ibid.*

65. *Ibid.*, p. 223

66. *BE*, p. 115

'There are no empirical grounds for historical optimism.'[67] For Berdyaev, the goal of history, the universal realization of Godmanhood or the full manifestation of the kingdom of God, will be attained only beyond history eschatologically, and that it will be so attained is a matter of Christian faith. 'My faith in victory is eschatological and my religion is prophetic.'[68]

In the introduction to his book *The Wisdom of God* Father Sergey Bulgakov referred to the way in which a strong sense of the reality of God can encourage a turning away from the world and all its values to a one-sided preoccupation with transcendent reality, the wholly Other. The opposite attitude, Bulgakov maintained, finds expression in the secularization of life and in non-religious or anti-religious humanism. The doctrine of Godmanhood, however, combines belief in the reality of God with recognition of the value of creation, and it expresses a religious humanism. Bulgakov's claim seems to the present writer to be justified. To be sure, difficulties can be raised in regard to the idea of Godmanhood. Some would argue, for example, that it is an attempt to unite what cannot be united. But it can hardly be denied that the doctrine lies at the heart of Christianity and is central to Christian humanism. It was this Christian humanism which the Russian religious thinkers presented as an alternative to various forms of secular or non-religious humanism. In their view, it was idle to expect denial of the human being's relationship to God to contribute to the transformation of human society for the better.

67. *Ibid.*, p. 209
68. *Ibid.*, p. 253

Chapter 5

The concept of Sophia

As the doctrine of the Incarnation is affirmed in the Christian creeds, the idea of Godmanhood, at any rate as applying to Christ as the God-man *par excellence*, can reasonably be said to be familiar to all who have some knowledge of the Christian religion. Whether or not they believe in the Incarnation, the idea of Godmanhood is not likely to strike them as something entirely novel or strange. References, however, to Sophia or Sophiology are apt to appear mysterious, puzzling and obscure. Such references would presumably seem less obscure to a devout member of the Russian Orthodox Church, who was aware of, say, the icons of St Sophia, or Holy Wisdom, at Novgorod and Kiev, not to speak of the dedication of the great basilica at Constantinople. But for most westerners reference to Sophiology, if it suggests anything at all, is likely to conjure up the idea of some obscure esoteric doctrine, a product of theosophical or gnostic speculation, peripheral to the Christian faith or even a superfluous addition thereto.

For Solovyev, however, the idea of Sophia was connected with that of Godmanhood, and Sergey Bulgakov roundly asserted that Sophiology is nothing but the full elucidation of Godmanhood.[1] N.O. Lossky described Sophiology as 'a doctrine highly characteristic of Russian religious philosophy',[2] and Father Pavel Florensky (1892–1943?) went so far as to claim that the idea of Sophia, the divine Wisdom, was the determining characteristic of the Russian religious consciousness.[3]

1. WG, p.34

2. *History of Russian Philosophy*, p. 406

3. See *Pavel Florensky. A Metaphysics of Love*, by Robert Slesinski, p. 170 (New York, 1984).

Not all Russian religious thinkers have agreed with this contention. For example, Father George Florovsky (1893–1979), a well known Orthodox theologian, took a rather dim view of the Sophiology of Florensky and Bulgakov, and his attitude was shared by Vladimir Lossky, the son of N.O. Lossky. There is, however, no one single take-it-or-leave-it Sophiological theory. The theme was treated by different thinkers in somewhat different ways, one writer being more concerned than another with making his speculative thought harmonize with traditional Orthodox theology. For the matter of that, we cannot find one single consistent use of the word Sophia, or Wisdom, even in the writings of Solovyev, who is credited with being the first Russian religious philosopher to develop the subject. But even if the present writer possessed the requisite knowledge, it would not be possible to provide here a comprehensive treatment of the theme. Discussion will be confined to some selected aspects. As a start, I propose to outline some of the relevant ideas of Solovyev.

II

In the sapiential books of the Old Testament (at any rate in *Proverbs*, *Wisdom* and *Ecclesiasticus*) divine Wisdom, the Wisdom of God, is personified and referred to as 'she'. This personification doubtless encouraged the tendency in the Russian Orthodox Church to identify Wisdom with Mary, the Mother of God.[4] When Russian medieval cathedrals were dedicted to St Sophia, this tended to be regarded as equivalent to a dedication to the Theotokos, the Mother of God. With Solovyev, however, we at first find an interpretation of Sophia as the Eternal Feminine. As a boy of nine, Solovyev, while present at the Liturgy in a Moscow church, had a visionary experience of a 'beautiful lady', whom he was later to identify with the divine Wisdom. In 1875 he had another such experience, this time while pursuing research in the British Museum at London. He also heard a voice telling him to go to

4. Referring to G.P. Fedotov's idea of the Novgorodian concept of Sophia John Meyendorff remarks that 'it seems likely that until the sixteenth century the identification of Sophia with Christ was generally accepted as self-evident'. *The Russian Religious Mind*, Vol. 2, by G.P. Fedotov, edited by John Meyendorff, Cambridge (Mass.), 1966, p. 192, note 3.

Egypt, which he proceeded to do. While in the desert, he was captured, robbed and then released by a group of Bedouin. There ensued his third visionary experience of a beautiful lady. Reference is made to the three experiences in his poem 'Three Meetings'.

There is no need to spend time discussing the question whether Solovyev saw anything existing objectively 'out there'. When this sort of question was raised, he used to reply that even purely subjective experience can have meaning for the experiencer, and that it is this meaning which counts. In 'Three Meetings' he refers to Sophia, personified as the 'beautiful lady', as holding all things in one. According to Berdyaev, 'the vision of Sophia is the vision of the beauty of the divine cosmos, of the transfigured world'.[5] This vision of cosmic Beauty was a source of inspiration for symbolist poets such as Blok and Bely, an inspiration which found expression in, for example, Blok's 'Verses about the Beautiful Lady'. Whereas, however, the symbolist poets tended to introduce an element of the erotic into their references to the Eternal Feminine, it was not Solovyev's intention to exalt the earthly Aphrodite, nor did he suggest that Woman should be turned into an object of man's worship. In the preface to a collection of his poems he explained that what he had in mind was eternal Beauty, transcending the sphere of sense. Further, he saw his visionary experience as a call to explore the idea of total-unity and to work for the regeneration of mankind. The concept of Wisdom or Sophia came to play a conspicuous role in his developed metaphysics, being used to elucidate, or so he hoped, the relationship between God and the world.

In his *Lectures on Godmanhood* Solovyev says that in the divine being two unities have to be distinguished, the one active or productive, the other produced. The first is identified with the Logos, with God as active force, while the second, 'to which we have given the mystical name of Sophia, is the principle of humanity'.[6] By 'the principle of humanity' Solovyev means the archetypal and eternal idea of humanity, the ideal of humanity; he does not mean 'man as a phenomenon'[7] who is certainly not eternal. This archetypal idea or ideal, we are told, is

5. *The Russian Idea*, p. 176

6. *LG*, p. 174. From Lecture VIII.

7. *Ibid.*, p. 175

realized in the Christ, the God-man, so that 'Sophia is the ideal or perfect humanity, eternally contained in the integral divine being or Christ',[8]–in Christ, that is to say, as the eternal Word.

Description of Sophia as a produced unity, as an ideal archetype generated eternally in the Logos or Word, naturally suggests that Sophia should be conceived as being simply an idea, as inactive that is to say. According to Solovyev, however, Sophia, as ideal humanity, is also the active soul of the world and the active principle of the divine-human organism, the body of Christ. In so far as the world-soul is permeated by the divine total-unity, it can transmit this unity to creation, uniting the multiplicity of creatures with God. In other words, Sophia is conceived as a bridge or mediator between God and the world.

It is all very well, it may be said, to represent Sophia or the world-soul as actively bringing together into unity beings or elements which were previously disunited and disordered. The difficulty is to see how, if God is the Absolute, the total-unity, disunity and disorder can have arisen in the first place.

In order to answer this question Solovyev has recourse to the idea of a cosmic Fall. We are informed that 'the world-soul can herself choose the object of the striving of her life'[9] and even assert herself apart from God. By so acting she loses her unifying power over creation, and the 'universal organism becomes transformed into a mechanical aggregate of atoms'.[10] However, the Logos comes to the rescue, conferring upon the world-soul, as its determining form, the idea of total-unity. In dependence, therefore, upon the Logos the world-soul strives to realize the eternal idea in creation, performing a unifying function and progressively building up the divine-human organism, of which Christ is the centre. The development of this organism and the progressive realization of Godmanhood are one and the same thing.

We have just seen that Solovyev identifies Sophia with the world-soul considered as the active principle which progressively exemplifies in the created world the eternal all-uniting Idea in the Logos. But Sophia is

8. *Ibid.*, p. 174

9. *Ibid.*, p. 191. From Lecture IX.

10. *Ibid.*, p. 192

also identified with the end of this process, with what is produced, namely spiritualized humanity, the society of persons united in God-manhood. As far therefore as the *Lectures in Godmanhood* are concerned, Sophia is conceived in a variety of ways; as the eternal ideal archetype of humanity, as the world-soul considered as actively engaged in realizing this archetypal idea, and finally as the fully developed divine-human organism. Sophia is depicted both as the active principle of the creative process and as its realized goal, the kingdom of God, the society of those participating in Godmanhood.

Identification of Sophia with the world-soul was characteristic of Solovyev's *Lectures on Godmanhood*. In later writings, belonging to the period when he was more interested in the reunion of the Churches than in metaphysical speculation, identification of Sophia with the world-soul seems to have been quietly dropped. At any rate it lost all prominence. In *Russia and the Universal Church* Solovyev refers to 'the incarnate Sophia, whose central and completely personal manifestation is Jesus Christ, whose feminine complement is the Blessed Virgin, and whose universal extension is the Church'.[11] Thus Sophia is still conceived as 'the perfect society'[12], and we are told that the mission of 'the new Russia'[13] is to declare to the world this 'social incarnation of the Godhead in the Universal Church',[14] At the same time the embodiment of divine Wisdom in the universal Church is represented as an extension or prolongation of its embodiment in Jesus Christ. In other words, the context of the theory of Sophia is here formed more by Christian belief, devotion and hopes than by the complicated metaphysics of the *Lectures on Godmanhood*, a metaphysics heavily dependent on the Platonic tradition, on writers such as Jakob Boehme and Franz von Baader, and on German idealism, especially the philosophizing of Schelling. It is not a question of claiming that Solovyev abandoned or repudiated his metaphysics; it is more a question of a temporary shift of interest.

11. *Russia and the Universal Church*, p. 176

12. *Ibid.*, p. 212

13. *Ibid.*, p. 178

14. *Ibid.*

III

Perhaps a few brief comments would be appropriate at this point. They would at any rate provide some sort of breather.

The philosopher N.O. Lossky believed that in Solovyev's treatment of Sophiology 'there is vagueness and inconsistency'.[15] Sometimes Sophia is represented as being eternally perfect, while at another time Sophia is described as the world-soul which has fallen away from God and has to make her way back again. Again, sometimes Sophia is identified with an eternal, archetypal idea, sometimes with the world-soul, sometimes with the substance of God, and sometimes with the Mother or God. Obviously, Solovyev was free to change his mind if he thought it desirable. The trouble, however, is that different accounts occur in one and the same work, the *Lectures on Godmanhood*. It may be possible to present the different ways of speaking as complementary aspects of one coherrent and self-consistent whole, but, even if it is possible, the task was not performed by Solovyev himself, who tends to leave his readers wondering how precisely Sophia is supposed to be conceived.

Lossky's claim that Solovyev's treatment of Sophiology was vague and inconsistent seems to me substantially justified. One might add the following line of criticism, namely that Solovyev imparts to his readers information about such matters as the world-soul and its doings without offering much evidence to show that things are as he says they are. It would, of course, be an exaggeration to assert that in his *Lectures* Solovyev never argues in support of the truth of his assertions. As has already been mentioned, he tries to develop a systematic deduction of his philosophical version of the Christian doctrine of the Trinity. He also tries to deduce the necessity of creation and the Incarnation. None the less, the reader is likely to find himself wondering time and time again how Solovyev can be so confident that he knows this or that to be the case. It is true that his assertions do not come simply out of the blue; they have their backgrounds, whether in Scripture or in the historical development of religious and metaphysical thought. But the western reader at any rate can hardly avoid the impression of being treated to a series of assertions which are certainly not unquestionable.

15. *History of Russian Philosophy*, p. 131

Such criticism does not, of course, alter the fact that, though the concept of divine Wisdom (as far as Christian thought is concerned) was of Biblical origin, Sophiology as a theological-philosophical theory was to all intents and purposes a creation of Solovyev. His main successors in this field were two theologians, Pavel Florensky and Sergey Bulgakov. They shared Solovyev's view of the importance of Sophiology, but they also tried to free it from what they considered to be the blemishes or questionable features in Solovyev's presentation. An attempt of this nature had already been made by Prince Evgeny Trubetskoy, but the present writer intends to confine his attention to Florensky and Bulgakov.

IV

Born in 1892, Florensky studied mathematics at the University of Moscow. Besides being a brilliant mathematician, he was also a physicist. After graduating in 1904, he declined the university's offer of a scholarship which would have enabled him to pursue research in the field of mathematics and, instead, began studying in the Moscow Theological Academy. In 1911 he was ordained priest. After acceptance of a dissertation *On Spiritual Truth* he was appointed a professor in the Academy. His main work, *The Pillar and Foundation of Truth*, which incorporated and amplified the earlier dissertation, was published at Moscow in 1914. For a time the Soviet authorities found him useful as a lecturer and writer in various scientific areas, such as electrical engineering, and also as an inventor. Thus in 1927 he invented an oil to which the name 'dekanite' was given to mark the completion of ten years under the new regime. But as he steadfastly refused to abandon the priesthood and even turned up to lecture in his clerical dress, the authorities eventually lost patience and imprisoned him in 1933. He seems to have died in a labour camp in 1943.

Florensky maintained that the concept of Sophia was not the product of metaphysical speculation but had been generated by the Orthodox religious consciousness, of which it was a determining characteristic. He appealed to the evidence of icons and to the seventeenth-century liturgical Office in honour of Sophia as divine Wisdom at Novgorod (for the feast of the Dormition of the Blessed Virgin on 15 August), the text of which he had printed in a periodical in 1912. In claiming that the concept of divine Wisdom had a basis in religious belief and devotion Florensky was doubtless justified, even if he sometimes tended to go well beyond the available evidence. At any rate his claims bear witness to the importance which he himself attached to Sophiology.

In Christian thought, according to Florensky, Sophia was first conceived as identical with the Logos or Word of God, while at a later stage, with the early Slavs, the idea became associated with the Mother of God, as filled with divine grace. Finally, interest became centred in the cosmological function of Sophia as the bridge or link between God and the world. It was presumably to this stage of thought that Berdyaev was referring when he remarked that the problem of Sophia, as stated by Florensky, 'was not one of the problems of traditional theology, however much Florensky tried to find support in the doctors of the Church'.[16] At the same time there are certainly some passages of the Bible (for example, in the eighth chapter of *Proverbs*) which, if understood literally, suggest the idea of Wisdom as exercising a mediating function between God and the world.

As Florensky conceived Sophia as the bridge between God and the world, he not unnaturally saw her as belonging to two levels of reality, the divine and the creaturely. As belonging to the heavenly sphere, Sophia is intimately related to the Logos or Word, being the thought-content of the divine mind.[17] Put in another way, Sophia is the archetype of creation and its transcendental unity. The divine thought, however, is creative, and Sophia exists in creatures as a kind of world-soul, present in all creatures and uniting them.

There are other ways too in which, according to Florensky, Sophia can be conceived. For example, as belonging to the heavenly sphere she can be described as God's creative love, while as belonging to the terrestrial sphere she is the realized love of God, the created manifestation of this love. Again, in her archetypal aspect Sophia can be conceived as the ideal Church, the heavenly Jerusalem, while she can also be conceived as the Church on earth, considered as comprising all

16. *The Russian Idea*, p. 239

17. *The Pillar and Foundation of Truth*, p. 326 (Moscow, 1914, reprinted in 1970 by Gregg International Publishers, Farnborough, UK).

human beings who are united with Christ by grace and thus are members of his mystical Body.

It is none too easy, it seems to me, to make out precisely what Florensky held. If Sophia were conceived simply as an intermediary being, distinct from God and yet not part of the created visible world, one might feel inclined to judge postulation of such a being superfluous, but at any rate there would not be any question of Sophia constituting an additional divine Person, additional to the Persons of the Trinity that is to say. When, however, we find Florensky describing Sophia as a fourth hypostatic element in the Trinity, it is natural to wonder whether a Quaternity is not being substituted for the traditional Trinity. If this interpretation is mistaken, what precisely has Florensky got in mind?

We are assured by Florensky that he conceives Sophia neither as a fourth Person of the Godhead nor as identical with the Logos, the second person of the Trinity, but as 'a non-consubstantial Person'.[18] That is to say, Sophia is not to be conceived as being of one substance with the Father, Son and Holy Spirit, though she participates in the divine life and creative activity. From this it seems to follow that Sophia is to be conceived as an intermediary being between the triune God and the multiplicity of creatures. Thus in his valuable book on Florensky's metaphysics Father Robert Slesinski quotes and apparently endorses a statement made by Archbishop Pitirim of Volokolamsk, namely that Sophia 'is something that exists and has real being, being neither God nor the world'.[19] When Slesinski says that, for Florensky, Sophia is 'no such independently existing intermediary',[20] he is engaged in defending Florensky from the accusation that he conceived Sophia as an *uncreated* intermediary. Sophia is a created, not an uncreated intermediary.

This is all very well, but if Sophia is a creature, distinct from God, can she reasonably be identified with the thought-content of the divine mind, with the archetypal idea of creation? Is not any such archetypal idea really one with God, with the Logos? And if, as we are told, Sophia is 'simply creation itself, it being coextensive and coterminous with all

18. *Ibid.*, p. 349

19. Slesinsky, p. 177. See note 3 above.

20. *Ibid.*, p. 193

created being',[21] are we not left with God on the one hand and the created world on the other? If, under one aspect, Sophia is one with God and, under her other aspect, one with creation, she can hardly be an intermediary being between God and creation. Presumably, however, she is to be looked on as a world-soul, of which it can be said that 'one in God, she is many in creation'.[22] As I have said, it is not altogether easy to make out precisely how Florensky's doctrine of Sophia should be understood.

If, as Florensky maintained, Sophiology had its original home in Orthodox devotion, in the Orthodox religious consciousness, such critical comments as the foregoing may seem tiresome and irrelevant. But inasmuch as Florensky attributed to Sophia a cosmic role and developed a theory, critical examination of his theoretical construction is certainly in order. We are hardly in a position to evaluate any Sophiological theory unless we are clear about the nature of the claims that are made. I readily admit, however, that there is a point of view from which the sort of critical points made above can understandably appear as heavy-handed and somewhat unfair. For if Florensky had been expelled from the Soviet Union in 1922 instead of being retained because of his abilities as mathematician and scientist, he would doubtless have had the opportunity to clarify his ideas and to develop them further. Father Slesinski does well to remind us that in comparison with Bulgakov 'Florensky merely sketches the rough features of Sophiology'.[23] So let us turn to Bulgakov.

V

After graduating from the University of Moscow in the Faculty of Law Sergey Nikolaevich Bulgakov taught political economy in the Technical School at Moscow. His two-volume work *Capitalism and Agriculture* was published in 1900, and in the following year he was appointed professor of political economy at Kiev. In 1906 he returned to Moscow to teach in the Institute of Commerce, and in 1917 he became professor

21. *Ibid.*, p. 194

22. *The Pillar and Foundation of Truth*, p. 329

23. Slesinski, p. 195

of political economy in the university. As already mentioned, he had
been for a time a 'Legal Marxist', but some divergence from orthodox
Marxism was already visible in his work on capitalism and agriculture.
His conversion to a belief in absolute values found expression in *From
Marxism to Idealism* (1903), and 'idealism' soon passed into religious
faith. He was a contributor to *Vekhi* (1909), and in 1911 he gave an
account of his religious conversion and defended a religious world-view
in *Two Cities*. In 1917 he published *The Unfading Light*, one of his
major religious writings. In the following year he was ordained priest.
For a short while he was professor of political economy and theology in
the University of Simferopol in the Crimea, but in 1921 he was deprived
of his chair, and in the following year he was expelled from the Soviet
Union. From 1925 until his death in 1944 he lived in Paris, where he
was professor of dogmatic theology at the Orthodox Theological
Institute, which he had helped to found. He was a prolific writer. His
view of the relationship between philosophy and theology was expressed in *The Theology of Philosophy* (1927). His *Philosophy of Language*
(more properly *Philosophy of the Name*) was published posthumously,
though it had been written in 1919. Here however, we are concerned
only with Bulgakov's theory of Sophia, the divine Wisdom.

In his writings Bulgakov pays tribute to Solovyev not only as his own
guide to Christ at a time when he, Bulgakov, was moving away from
Marxism, but also as 'the first Russian sophiologist'.[24] At the same time
he tells his readers that he does not share what he regards as Solovyev's
marked tendency to syncretism, the way in which Solovyev draws both
on ancient gnostic systems and on the writings of western thinkers such
as Boehme. Bulgakov also finds fault with Solovyev's poetic mysticism,
as being out of tune with the Orthodox tradition and as having
contributed to the erotic attitude manifested by Blok and Bely to the
Eternal Feminine. In other words, Bulgakov intends to develop Sophiology in accordance with a strictly Orthodox line of thought, and he
credits Florensky with having put 'the problem of sophiology in an
absolutely Orthodox setting'.[25] According to Bulgakov Sophiology
threatens none of the dogmas of the Orthodox Church.

24. *WG*, p. 23

25. *Ibid.*, p. 25

As one might expect, in view of the thought of Solovyev and Florensky, the point of departure for Bulgakov's Sophiological speculation is the relation between God and the world or, 'what is practically the same thing, between *God* and *man*'.[26] In cosmological or metaphysical thinking, Bulgakov tells us, there are two extreme positions, monism, in which the distinction between God and the world vanishes, and dualism, in which an unbridgeable chasm is postulated between the transcendent God, the wholly Other, and finite beings, creatures. Similarly, in the attitudes of Christians to life we can discern two poles, two opposed positions, a world-denying escapism on the one hand and, on the other, a faint-hearted submission or capitulation to the standards and values of 'the world'. In general, there has been a strong tendency to confront human beings with a choice, 'God *or* the world, 'God *or* man'. The alternative to such dichotomies, Bulgakov maintains, is the doctrine of Godmanhood, and this is 'the main theme of Sophiology, which in fact represents nothing but its full dogmatic elucidation'.[27] It is the theory of Sophia which enables us to overcome the sharp dichotomy between God and the world without thereby committing ourselves to monism.

Bulgakov's theory of Sophia is substantially similar to that of Florensky. Sophia is located, so to speak, on both sides of the divide, having both divine and creaturely, heavenly and terrestrial aspects. In *The Unfading Light* Sophia is said to be the divine Idea and the object of God's love. She is also said to return this love. It may therefore seem that Sophia is identified by Bulgakov with the Logos or Word of God. But this is not his intention. The Logos is conceived as active, whereas Sophia is conceived as receptive, as surrendering herself in love and as thus being the Eternal Feminine. In relation to the world, however, Sophia, the divine Idea, unites in herself the ideas of all creatures and can be described as the soul of the world and as '*natura naturans* in relation to *natura naturata*'.[28] According to Bulgakov, the substratum

26. *Ibid.*, p. 30

27. *Ibid.*, p. 84

28. *The Unfading Light (Svet nevechernii)*, pp. 213 and 223 (Moscow, 1917; Gregg International Publishers, Farnborough, 1971).

of created things is universal matter. The original nothing was transformed by God's creative power into the 'unlimited' of early Greek
philosophy, formation of the various levels of creation being the
progressive actualization of the potentialities of matter. This process
takes place under the guidance of Sophia as 'the soul of the world, the
anima mundi',[29] bringing light into darkness.

Considered in her divine aspect, Sophia is said to transcend creation.
But although she is conceived as a heavenly reality, Bulgakov, like
Florensky, insists that she is not a fourth Person of the Trinity. As for
Sophia in her terrestrial aspect, she is said to function as the world-soul.
Inasmuch as 'the unlimited' contains in itself the potential entelechies or
immanent 'ideas' of things, it can be said to possess Sophian elements.
Actualized and taken together as a unity, they reflect the divine Idea,
the heavenly Sophia, and constitute her terrestrial aspect.

Published in 1917, *The Unfading Light* was an early work. Bulgakov
developed his theory of Sophia in later writings, particularly in *The
Lamb of God* (*Agnus Dei*, 1933), *The Comforter* (1936) and *The Bride
of the Lamb* (1945), being respectively parts one, two and three of the
work *On Godmanhood*. It is, of course, this developed Sophiology
which is summarized in *The Wisdom of God* (1937), the English
translation of the outline of Sophiology which appeared while the third
volume of *On Godmanhood* (the volume dealing with eschatology) was
being prepared for publication (though it was not published until after
Bulgakov's death).

A notable development in Bulgakov's account of Sophia is his explicit
identification of the heavenly Sophia with the substance or nature of
God. This nature, the Godhead of God so to speak, is said to belong
equally to each of the three Persons of the Trinity but not to be itself a
Person, a fourth Person. God (in the sense of the three Persons) is said
to love Sophia as the divine self-manifestation, and Sophia is said to
love God. 'If God loves Sophia, Sophia also loves God'.[30] Though,
however, Sophia, as the divine substance or essence, must be possessed
equally by the three Persons, Bulgakov assures us that each possesses it

29. *Ibid.*, p. 223

30. *WG.* p. 58

in a special way. For example, it is the Logos, the second Person, who determines 'the *content* of Sophia, as of the ideal *all*'.[31] That is to say, it is as possessed by the Logos that Sophia is the divine Idea, the unity of all archetypes.

As the divine Idea, the self-revelation of the Logos or Word, Sophia is said to be the prototype of creation, embracing in herself all the ideal forms of created beings. 'This means that the species of created beings do not represent some new type of forms, devised by God, so to speak, *ad hoc*, but that they are based upon eternal, divine prototypes'.[32] The world itself is God's creature, created out of nothing, but it comes to reflect the eternal archetypal ideas only through the operation of Sophia in her creaturely aspect, functioning, that is to say, as the soul of the world. Bulgakov describes the creaturely Sophia as the entelechy of the created world, the principle which actualizes itself in the course of the cosmic process.[33]

In spite of the fact that Bulgakov speaks of the divine and the created or creaturely Sophia, he insists that they should not be conceived as two independently existing realities. When God mirrored himself in non-being, 'the divine Sophia became the created Sophia'.[3] To put the matter in another way, the divine and the created Sophia are identical in content, though not in the manner of their being. The former exists as prototype, the latter as antitype. 'Remaining one, it [Sophia] exists in two modes, eternal and temporal, divine and creaturely.'[35] Between the heavenly and the terrestrial Sophia there is at one and the same time both identity and distinction.

What about human beings? Man was created in the image or likeness of a divine prototype, and though the Fall[36] obscured this likeness, it did not obliterate it. The human being thus retained the potentiality for

31. *Ibid.*, p. 76

32. *Ibid.*, p. 107

33. *Ibid.*, p. 114

34. *Agnus Dei*, p. 149 (Paris, YMCA Press, 1933). Cf. pp. 222 f. and 258.

35. *WG*, p. 121

36. Bulgakov's idea of the Fall was more in accordance with traditional theology than Solovyev's had been.

being reunited with God. But thus reunion takes place 'only in Godmanhood, in the Incarnation of the Word and outpouring of the Holy Spirit'.[37] Godmanhood is described by Bulgakov as 'the unity of eternal and created manhood which is Sophia, the Wisdom of God'.[38] When Bulgakov refers to eternal manhood, he is thinking, of course, of the archetypal idea or prototype of humanity. He conceives Godmanhood as the unity of divine and created Wisdom, a unity in distinction.

As one might expect, Bulgakov also identifies Sophia with the Church, considered as the extension of the Incarnation. Drawing a distinction between the Church as eternal, as prototypal, and the Church as empirically existing on earth, he identifies the former with Sophia in her divine aspect and the latter with Sophia in her creaturely aspect. He adds, however, that 'in the Church the two aspects of Wisdom mutually permeate one another and are entirely, inseparably and unconfusedly united'.[39] The Church on earth, needless to say, develops in time, and Bulgakov looks forward to the eventual manifestation of Godmanhood in all humanity. 'The freedom of the rebellious creature cannot stand out to the end against the divine Wisdom'.[40] When the process of 'deification' has reached its completion, God will be, in St Paul's words, 'all in all'.[41]

In outlining Bulgakov's theory of Sophia, we have frequently referred to Sophia as 'she'. This was the practice of Bulgakov himself. It may be as well, therefore, to repeat that he did not claim that Sophia is a person. As we have noted, he was careful to deny that Sophia in her divine aspect is a fourth divine Person. He also explained that the description of Sophia in her creaturely aspect as the soul of the world should not be understood as implying that this world-soul is personal. There is, it is true, a sense in which Sophia in her creaturely aspect is personal, but she is personalized not in herself but in human beings, human persons. Bulgakov does indeed associate both aspects of Sophia

---

37. *WG*, p. 121

38. *Ibid.*, p. 134

39. *Ibid.*, p. 201

40. *Ibid.*, p. 219

41. I *Corinthians*, XV, 28

in a special way with the Blessed Virgin as Mother of God, Theotokos, but it is Mary, not Sophia, who is a person. Obviously the use of feminine pronouns, such as 'she', inevitably suggests that Sophia is being conceived as a person. But this is all the more reason for reminding ourselves that Bulgakov repudiates any attempt to convert the Trinity into a Quaternity. As far as he was concerned, his Sophiology developed but did not contradict Orthodox theology.

VI

However this may be, in 1935 Bulgakov's Sophiology incurred censure from two quarters, one being the Metropolitan Sergius of Moscow (to be elected Patriarch in 1943), the other a synod of Orthodox bishops at Karlovci in Yugoslavia. Bulgakov thereupon addressed a memorandum to the Metropolitan Evlogy of Paris, in which he protested his orthodoxy. Evlogy supported him.

It is hardly necessary to say that Bulgakov's Orthodox critics did not object to the concept of divine Wisdom as such, nor to every devotional use of the idea. It was to some of his speculative theological and philosophical theories that they took exception. There were two main grounds for complaint. One accusation was that Bulgakov made of Sophia a fourth Person of the Trinity. The other line of criticism was that his thought was pantheistic, stating or at any rate implying an identity between God and the world.

In regard to the first objection, we have already seen that Bulgakov denied representing Sophia as a fourth Person of the Trinity. Sophia was located, so to speak, on a lower rung of the ladder or hierarchy of being. At the same time Bulgakov identified Sophia in her divine aspect with the substance or nature of God, the nature which is possessed by each of the three Persons, who are thus said to be consubstantial. If therefore Sophia is conceived as subordinate to or lower than the three Persons, it seems to follow that the divine substance or nature is subordinate to or lower than the three Persons. And this is not a view of the matter which is likely to win favour in the eyes of conservative theologians or prelates on the look-out for unwelcome novelties.

As for the charge of pantheism, Bulgakov maintained in reply that what he asserted was not the identity of God and the world but that nothing can exist outside God, as external to him. In other words, he expounded not pantheism but panentheism, the latter being not only compatible with orthodox belief but also part of the genuine Christian world-view.

Let us take it that Florensky and Bulgakov did not postulate two Sophias but only one, this one Sophia having two aspects, heavenly and terrestrial. Perhaps we can speak of two functions, an archetypal function on the one hand and a unifying function in creation on the other. The question arises whether this one Sophia is an intermediary being between God and the world. A good deal of what is said by Florensky and Bulgakov implies that this is indeed the case. That is to say, Sophia is an intermediary being which acts as a bridge or link between God and the world. But we also find it implied that in her heavenly or divine aspect Sophia is one with God, identifiable in fact with the divine substance or nature, while in her terrestrial or creaturely aspect Sophia is not distinct from creation. If therefore Sophia is one being or reality, it seems to follow that God and the world are one, or that God and the world are two aspects of one reality, the total-unity.

Obviously, neither Florensky nor Bulgakov had any intention of interpreting the word 'God' simply as a name for the world in which we find ourselves, the empirical world. At the same time the objections levelled against Bulgakov's Sophiology were not all captious or carping. As we have noted, the two theologians denied that they conceived Sophia as an uncreated intermediary being, existing independently of God. If, however, Sophia is a created being, it surely belongs to creation, rather than existing as an intermediary between God and creation. If, however, Sophia has two aspects, one of which is not distinct from God while the other is not distinct from the created world, it is difficult to avoid the conclusion that God and the created world are not distinct. In other words, it is not altogether a simple matter to distinguish clearly between the panentheism which Bulgakov affirms and the pantheism which he rejects.

Florensky referred to his theorizing as necessarily employing 'miserable schemata for what is experienced in the soul',[41] and he insisted that

---

42. *The Pillar and Foundation of Truth*, p. 324. Slesinski draws attention to this passage on p. 73 of his book.

truths derived from religious experience cannot be expressed conceptually without the use of antinomies. Though we can sympathize with
Florensky's feeling of the inadequacy of language to express what he
believed to be rooted in religious experience, however, it remains true
that the process of trying to communicate what one believes to be a
truth puts what one says in the public domain, so to speak, and exposes
it to critical examination. To some people such critical examination
doubtless seems unsympathetic and tiresome, perhaps even irrelevant.
Apart from Florensky's claim that Sophiology is rooted in the Orthodox religious consciousness, is it not in large part a sustained attempt to
express in philosophical and theological terms what is said about divine
Wisdom in the Bible? And have we the right to expect that the results
should exemplify the standards of clarity and precision on which the
rationalist mind likes to insist, especially when it is a question of ideas
which it is quite unprepared to consider seriously? After all, it is not as
though either Florensky or Bulgakov made no attempt to clarify their
ideas by approaching the theme from various angles and suggesting
different aspects of the subject. Rather than sniping at their statements
and complaining about lack of clarity and precision, would it not be
more helpful to contribute in a more positive way to the development of
Sophiology? If God is conceived as the wholly Other in a sense which
postulates an unbridgeable chasm between him and the world, creation
becomes unintelligible and the possibility of Godmanhood, of the
Incarnation and the elevation of the human being to union with God
through Christ is excluded from the start. For if Godmanhood is a real
possibility, the chasm between God and creation, God and the human
being, cannot be unbridgeable. The Sophiologists saw this clearly
enough, and if what they say lacks precision, the appropriate course is
to try to improve on their performance.

Given certain presuppositions, this is a reasonable point of view. But
it does not seem to be obvious that the concept of creation is
substantially clarified by introducing the idea of an intermediary being,
namely Sophia. Nor is it clear, in my opinion, that in treating of the
spiritualization of humanity the theologian cannot get on well enough
with the doctrines of the Incarnation and the indwelling of the Holy
Spirit. There is, of course, the talk about Sophia in certain books of the
Bible. But is it not perhaps sufficient to conceive Wisdom as a divine

attribute? To ask such questions is admittedly to show a lack of sympathy with Sophiology. But it is legitimate to wonder whether such speculation really fulfils the function which its sponsors claim that it does. From the historical point of view, Sophiology has certainly played a conspicuous role in Russian religious thought from Solovyev to Bulgakov, but I doubt whether it is an essential element in the doctrine of Godmanhood.

Speaking of Sophiology Berdyaev remarked that 'it is not clear what ought to be referred to revelation, what to theology and what to philosophy'.[43] In addition he drew attention, as one might expect, to the fact that Sophia, and not human freedom, was Bulgakov's 'fundamental idea'.[44] In Berdyaev's opinion, Bulgakov was too much given to representing human history as an advance, directed by Sophia. At the same time Berdyaev recognized that the theme of 'the divine in the created world'[45] was a central topic of much Russian religious thought, and he paid tribute to Bulgakov for 'his belief in the divine principle in man'.[46]

By way of conclusion, let me refer to an article on Russian Sophiology which appeared in a *Samizdat* publication in the Soviet Union in the year 1978[47]. In a note the author of the article, Viktor Kapitanchuk, remarks that one should distinguish between the very broad concept of Sophia expounded by Bulgakov and the narrower one employed by the author in his article, namely as the world of eternal divine ideas.[48]

43. *The Russian Idea*, p. 241

44. *Ibid.*

45. *Ibid.*, p. 240

46. *Ibid.*, p. 242

47. The article, entitled 'Ontologicheskaya problema v russkoi sofiologii', is included in *Obshchina*, No. 2 (1978). This publication is preserved in the archives of Keston College Library, and I am indebted to the Librarian of the College for kindly providing me with a photocopy of the article.

48. P. 111, note 12

Chapter 6

Athens or Jerusalem

In his *Lectures on Godmanhood* Solovyev asserted that in addition to religious faith and religious experience there was a need for religious thought, the product of this combination being philosophy of religion, understood as 'the *organization* of religious experience into an integrated, logically connected system'.[1] Solovyev's own philosophy can be regarded as a sustained attempt to perform this service for Christian faith and experience. It was a process of thought within Christianity, not external to it. At the same time Solovyev's way of going about things was seen by some critics as constituting in effect a take-over bid by philosophy, as an endeavour, that is to say, to transform Christian beliefs, derived from divine revelation and accepted in faith, into conclusions of metaphysical speculation.

This was the point of view of the writer Leon Shestov (Lev Isaakovich Schwarzman, 1866–1938), who emigrated from Russia in 1919 and eventually settled in Paris. In a long article entitled 'Speculation and Apocalypse', which appeared in two numbers of a Russian-language periodical for 1927–8, he paid tribute to Solovyev's talents as 'the first Russian religious philosopher'. He then went on to assert that, in the process of developing a religious philosophy, Solovyev, though without being aware of the fact, 'lured religion ...into the same trap into which Kant once lured metaphysics'.[3] When Kant persuaded or at any rate

1. *LG*, p. 107. From Lecture III.

2. *Speculation and Revelation*, translated by Bernard Martin, p. 19 (Athens, Ohio, 1982). This work is a translation of a collection of essays by Shestov entitled *Umozrenie i otkrovenie* (Paris, 1964). This translation will be referred to in notes as *SR*.

3. *Ibid.*, p. 22

invited metaphysics to try to justify itself before the tribunal of reason,
it was soon revealed as lacking any right to exist. Similarly, 'once
religion must justify itself ...its cause is in a bad way'.[4]

This line of thought did not proceed from any hostility to religion on
Shestov's part. On the contrary, he was a passionate God-seeker. What
he was attacking was any claim by philosophy to be qualified for sitting
in judgement on religion. In his view, any attempt to induce religion to
justify itself before the tribunal of reason led inevitably to the 'autocracy of reason',[5] to the complete victory of reason over religion. In his
philosophy of mythology and revelation Schelling had subordinated
religion to philosophy, and Solovyev followed suit. The difference
between them, according to Shestov, was that 'Schelling never believed
in his philosophy of revelation',[6] his sole concern being to overcome the
influence of Hegel, whereas Solovyev, though misguided, was perfectly
sincere, not noticing how, in his thought, philosophy had come to take
the place of revelation. It is true that towards the end of his life
Solovyev came to feel or divine that the 'eternal and final truth'[7] is
revealed not through philosophical reflection but through thunder and
lightning, as on Sinai. Yet even in the work which he left unfinished at
his death he maintained that for the philosopher nothing was more
desirable than truth tested through thinking. Solovyev's premises forced
him, even against his will, 'to seek for the biblical God a more perfect
successor who corresponds better to the demands of reason'.[8] In other
words, the Absolute tended to take the place of the biblical God.

Obviously, when Shestov criticized Solovyev, for whom he felt a
genuine admiration, he was attacking a certain line of thought and
proclaiming a different one, one which was presented in books and
essays which were not specifically directed against the thought of
Solovyev. It is with Shestov's general line of thought that we are
primarily concerned in this chapter. It is, of course, an ambiguous or

4. *Ibid.*, p. 21

5. *Ibid.*, p. 41

6. *Ibid.*, p. 31

7. *SR*, p.88

8. *Ibid.*, p. 79

two-faced line of thought. That is to say, a rationalist would see in it a clear admission that religion is 'irrational'. But Shestov was not unaware of this possibility. For him, as for Kierkegaard, faith was a venture, a flight beyond the limits of what the rationalist would be prepared to describe as 'rational'.

II

There was a constant theme running through Shestov's writings, so much so that he was accused of continually repeating himself. Even in his first book *Shakespeare and his Critic Brandes* (1897) he attacked rationalist philosophy, from Aristotle onwards, on the ground that it tried to subject reality and human life and experience to the schemata and demands of man's reason. The rationalist philosopher, as conceived by Shestov, interpreted and evaluated life in terms of thought, whereas Shakespeare saw life in its richness and knew very well that it could not be equated with thought. As time went on, this line of criticism of western rationalism came to take the form of a sharp antithesis between reason and faith, between speculative philosophy or metaphysics on the one hand and biblical revelation on the other. In his last work *Athens and Jerusalem* Shestov maintained that is was necessary to choose between Athens (philosophy) and Jerusalem (religious faith). One might choose either, but not both, as they are incompatible.

The issue can be clarified in this way. Shestov conceived rationalist philosophy as trying, in the interests of understanding or of obtaining conceptual mastery over the object of thought, to show how all reality is subject to law, to the reign of necessity. This involved either minimization or outright denial of human freedom. It also meant that limits had to be placed to the possibilities open to divine action. For example, although God was described as omnipotent, in rationalist philosophy, if God was admitted at all, he was conceived as subject to the law of non-contradiction. In effect, he was conceived as unable to do anything the thought of which was repugnant to the human reason. Thus man's reason was made the measure of all things.

Shestov rebelled against the idea that all is subject to the universal reign of necessity to the exclusion of freedom. At first emphasis was laid more upon human freedom, but later it was placed more on the unlimited freedom of God. This shift of emphasis, however, does not indicate any weakening of Shestov's belief in human freedom. It is a matter of his having become more and more preoccupied with the question whether we have to accept Spinoza's concept of God, which means accepting the universal reign of necessity, affecting both the totality and its constituent members, including human beings, or whether we choose to pin our faith to the God of Abraham, Isaac and Jacob, the God of biblical revelation. If the ultimate reality is the biblical God, the human being, made in the image of God, is also free. But if the God of Spinoza is the ultimate reality, the human being cannot be free. It is only if God transcends the reign of law as conceived in rationalist philosophy, that the human being can attain salvation from God. 'Freedom comes to man not from knowledge but from faith, which puts an end to all our fears'.[9]

III

As Shestov was passionately concerned with the preservation of faith and of belief in freedom, regarding this as a matter of life and death, and as he was given to underlining contrasts and emphasizing antitheses, disdaining compromise and dialectical reconciliation or harmonization of opposites, it is hardly surprising if he sometimes tends to give the impression of being a sworn foe of reason as such. It is desirable, however, to correct this sort of impression. As we have noted, Shestov was convinced that if reason is encouraged to invade the sphere of faith, the latter's death would soon follow. Further, he saw the human reason as aspiring to subject the whole of reality to the reign of necessity, excluding all freedom, whether of God or man. This aspiration he vehemently opposed. But he did not condemn reason as such; he was not so foolish as to deny that it has any useful function to perform in human life.

In an early work *The Apotheosis of Groundlessness* (1905) Shestov remarks that in the streets of life there is no electric light, no gas, not

9. *Ibid.*, p. 266

even a kerosene lamp.[10] If such things are to exist, they must be invented. Reasoning is required for everyday life and for the development of science. Further, as Shestov was to say in his last work, 'if you wish to have a solidly established science, you must place it under the protection of the idea of Necessity'.[11] We can have no science without the formulation of laws which make prediction possible. However, though Shestov recognizes the practical value and functions of science, he goes on to praise David Hume for seeing that in the world itself there is no necessity, but that necessity is read into the world, so to speak, by the human reason. The pragmatic value of science should not blind us to the fact that the law-governed world of science, a world in which necessity reigns, is the creation of the human reason. Generally speaking at any rate, philosophers have been seduced by the idea of universal and necessary truths. Hume, however, recognized these truths as what they really are, namely useful 'fictions', as Nietzsche was later to maintain.

The objection may be raised that, though Shestov was certainly not so eccentric as to maintain that mankind would be better off if all science were scrapped, he surely attacked philosophy as such. For if he really believed that 'the task of philosophy consists in teaching men to submit joyously to Necessity which hears nothing and is indifferent to all',[12] he can hardly have had a high opinion of philosophical reflection. Must he not have regarded it as an enemy of the human race?

It is true, of course, that Shestov repeatedly criticized philosophy and philosophers, but it would be an exaggeration to claim that he condemned all philosophical thought whatsoever. For one thing, when Hume questioned the belief that there are necessary relations existing 'out there' between things in the world, and when Nietzsche proposed

10. *All Things are Possible and Penultimate Words and Other Essays*, with a new introduction by Bernard Martin, p. 7 (Athens, Ohio, 1977). *All Things are Possible* is an English translation by S.S. Koteliansky of Shestov's *The Apotheosis of Groundlessness*. This translation was originally published at London and New York in 1920. In notes references to *ATP* are to Bernard Martin's volume.

11. *Athens and Jerusalem*, translated, with an introduction, by Bernard Martin, p. 82 (Athens, Ohio, 1966). This translation will be referred to in notes as *AJ*.

12. *Ibid.*, p. 80

the theory that even the basic principles of logic are biologically useful
fictions rather than eternal and necessary truths (lines of thought which
won Shestov's approval), both men were clearly philosophizing. For
another thing, Shestov was quite prepared to attribute a positive
function to the sort of critical philosophizing to which we have just
referred. 'The business of philosophy is to teach men to live in
uncertainty—man who is supremely afraid of uncertainty, and who is
forever hiding himself behind this or the other dogma'.[13] Philosophy is
represented as questioning and undermining alleged certainties, but this
process has, or should have, the positive function of showing people
how to live in the absence of these certainties.

Berdyaev, who was a friend of Shestov at Paris and who respected
him as 'a philosopher who philosophized with his whole being'[14]
remarked that Shestov made use of philosophy to attack philosophy[15].
Well, so he did of course; but it was a particular kind of philosophy
which he attacked. To be sure, he sometimes referred to his target of
attack as 'rational philosophy', a phrase which prompts one to ask how
there can be any other kind of philosophy. But the target was also, and
less misleadingly described as 'rationalist philosophy', 'metaphysics'
and 'speculative philosophy'. In a review of two works by Richard
Kroner, Shestov asserted that 'the essence of rationalism consists in
man's profound conviction that it is given to his "thinking" to reveal
the essence of the universe, to grasp its depths and to take possession of
all its treasures, as Hegel said in his inaugural address at the University
of Berlin'.[16] Obviously, by 'metaphysics' and 'speculative philosophy'
as objects of attack Shestov meant much the same as he meant by
'rationalist philosophy'. He conceived speculative philosophy or
metaphysics as a philosophy of total-unity, aspiring to comprehend
everything in terms of the categories of the human reason. Any such
philosophy, he believed, tries to subject everyone and everything to the
reign of necessity, so that all events, including human choices, are

---

13. *ATP*, p. 12

14. *SR*, p. 1. From an appreciaton written by Berdyaev after Shestov's death.
15. *DR*, p. 88

16. *SR*. p. 104

predictable in principle. The unpredictable escapes the dominion of reason and cannot be admitted as constituting a feature of reality.

IV

We have noted that Shestov attributed to philosophy, in the sense or senses in which he approved of philosophy, the positive function of teaching people how to live in the midst of uncertainty. But this positive task can hardly be performed by the philosophizing which consists in the questioning and undermining of cherished beliefs and alleged certainties. Humean criticism alone, for example, does not teach one how to live. Something more is required. This Shestov found in what he described sometimes as 'biblical philosophy', sometimes as 'Judaeo-Christian philosophy' and sometimes as 'religious philosophy', and which he opposed to 'speculative philosophy'. We have indeed seen that he rejected religious philosophy (or philosophy of religion) as conceived by Solovyev, on the ground it was a flagrant example of speculative philosophy transforming religion into itself. But by religious philosophy in the sense in which he identified it with biblical philosophy and approved of it he meant 'not a search for the eternal structure and order of immutable being ...[but] a turning away from knowledge and a surmounting by faith, in a boundless tension of all its forces, of the false fear of the unlimited will of the Creator ... To put it in another way, religious philosophy is the final supreme struggle to recover original freedom ...'.[17] Religious philosophy is therefore said by Shestov to introduce 'into our thought a new dimension—faith',[18] a dimension which speculative philosophy does its best to dispose of or obliterate.

The religious philosophy in question is conceived by Shestov as a struggle to overcome the tyranny of alleged eternal and necessary truths, and to recognize that with God all things are possible, that there are no limits to his freedom. This struggle involves leaving behind or transcending the God of the philosophers, the God of Spinoza or of Hegel, and embracing faith in the God of the Bible, the God of Abraham, Isaac and Jacob, who is able to do even what is said to be

17. *AJ*, p. 70
18. *Ibid*., p. 372

impossible. He can, as one might put it, wipe the slate clean and make all things new, undoing the past.

Judaeo-Christian philosophy as conceived by Shestov is thus far from being simply a critical assessment of the logical status of what are claimed to be necessarily true propositions, an assessment such as can be made by a professional logician who is innocent of any religious interests. For Shestov envisages an assessment of this kind as being carried on not simply for the sake of increasing our knowledge of logical relations but primarily in order to facilitate the leap of faith, faith in a God whose power is not limited by any rules formulated by the huma mind or reason. The process of thinking would be religiously oriented. In a discussion of some of Martin Buber's writings Shestov asserted that 'there was a moment in the history of the world when someone took freedom away from men and in its place foisted knowledge upon them', instilling into them 'the conviction that knowledge alone guarantees them freedom'.[19] In Shestov's opinion, knowledge is the source of bondage, not of freedom. To recover freedom it is necessary to transcend knowledge in the movement of religious faith.

Given this attitude on Shestov's part, it is natural to raise the question whether in phrases such as 'biblical philosophy' and 'religious philosophy', as employed by Shestov, use of the word 'philosophy' is justifiable. After all, Shestov is not recommending adoption of yet another system of speculative philosophy, one which he believes to be more genuinely religious than any already existing system. He roundly rejects speculative philosophy and substitutes the movement of religious faith, a movement which is said to transcend knowledge and the limits of what the human mind is accustomed to consider as rational. Whatever the value of this movement may be, can it be properly described as philosophy or philosophizing?

Some light is shed on the meaning which Shestov attaches to the word 'philosophy' by a passage in his book *In Job's Balances*. We are told that 'the best and only complete definition of philosophy'[20] was given by Plotinus when he said that philosophy is concerned with what

19. *SR*, p. 116

20. *JB*, p. 31

matters most, with what is most valuable or most to be prized. This definition, Shestov maintains, serves to distinguish philosophy from science, inasmuch as science eschews value-judgments and does not even raise the question whether something 'matters' or not. At the same time the definition does away with the barriers which separate or are thought to separate philosophy from religion and art. For both the artist and the religious prophet are concerned with what matters most in human life or with what is most to be prized. Obviously, Shestov's pronouncements relating to science, art and philosophy are open to critical discussion. But his line of thought does make his use of the word 'philosophy' somewhat clearer. In his view, religious faith is of supreme value for life, and thinking which is oriented to and facilitates the leap of faith can be described as 'philosophical' in terms of the Plotinian definition.

When providing some idea of the nature of what he understands by 'biblical philosophy'. Shestov pursues certain frequently recurring themes, and I wish to give a rather fuller account of some of them. Let us start with the idea of God as enjoying unlimited freedom.

V

As has already been remarked, Shestov saw science as trying to show that the world is subject to the reign of necessity, that determining causality operates throughout, and that in principle all events and choices are predictable. In such a world, Shestov argued, God is no longer conceived as capable of intervening, of changing anything, and is progressively relegated to the world's periphery. Someone might perhaps feel prompted to suggest that, if God is identified with the world, he is far from being relegated to the periphery, He is very much in the centre of things, even if the identification means that necessity reigns throughout reality. Shestov, however, makes a sharp retort to any such suggestion. 'It should be clear even to the blind that the equation, God = nature = substance, ought to mean that we need not and must not allow God any further place in philosophy.'[21] In other words, Schopenhauer was right when he claimed that pantheism is

21. *Ibid.*, p. xviii

simply a polite form of atheism. In Shestov's opinion, Spinoza was lying when he wrote to a correspondent that in his system God was given the same place of honour as in other systems. Retention of a word is not enough to mask absence of the reality.

Instead of tamely endorsing the idea of the world as subject to the reign of necessity, philosophy should, according to Shestov, make it clear that this picture of the world is not a reliable portrait, nor a photograph, but rather a mental construction, undoubtedly useful for certain purposes but none the less a man-made construction. In the connection Shestov makes use of the word 'metaphysics' to refer to an activity of which he approves. 'Metaphysics,' we are told, 'has not given us a single truth obligatory upon all. That is true, but it is not an objection to metaphysics.'[22] There may even be a sense in which metaphysics is 'more useful and more important than the positive sciences'[23]. What is this sense? Metaphysics, Shestov suggests, has the task of 'devaluating the truths of the positive sciences, along with the very idea of constraint as the sign of truth'.[24] Evidently, Shestov is not trying to reinstate the dogmatic metaphysics which Kant submitted to adverse criticism. He is here applying the word 'metaphysics' to the activity of debunking the idea of necessary and eternal truths and universal, inviolable laws. To use the word in this sense does not conduce to clarity, but at any rate it does not mean that Shestov has suddenly become an enthusiast for 'speculative philosophy'.

Once the truth has been grasped that the world of science is a construction of the human mind, possessing pragmatic value but not expressing eternal truth, room is made for divine intervention in the world and in human history. To be sure, the premise that the scientific view of the world is a useful fiction does not entail the conclusion that God exists. But Shestov did not claim to be able to prove that God exists. In his view, the Bible knows nothing of such proofs and does not concern itself with them. His conviction was that, when the concept of the world as subject to the reign of necessity has been shown to be a

22. *AJ*, p. 428
23. *Ibid.*
24. *Ibid.*

construction of the human mind, the way has been opened up for biblical faith in the omnipotent God to reassert itself.

In the Middle Ages the ascription of omnipotence to God was commonly interpreted as meaning that God, creator and lord of all things, could do anything which did not involve contradiction. There were, of course, some differences of opinion about what kinds of action would count as contradictory. Moreover, while some thinkers emphasized the idea of God acting only in accordance with his nature, others, especially in the late Middle Ages, were inclined to approach the matter from a more strictly logical point of view. But there is no need to enlarge upon this theme here. In the present context the relevant point is that Shestov conceived the medieval theologians and philosophers as implying that the principle of non-contradiction 'exists of itself and is independent of God',[25] as though the principle ruled God from outside, as it were. This interpretation is not in fact correct. The medieval theologians' general idea was that God can do anything, but that the self-contradictory is not and cannot be 'anything'. Shestov, however, asked where did medieval philosophy get 'this unshakable conviction that the principle of contradiction cannot be overcome? Not from the Bible, surely '.[26] The source of the conviction in question was Greek thought, not biblical revelation. True, it might have found a place in what Etienne Gilson liked to regard as 'Judaeo-Christian philosophy',[27] but it was alien to Judaeo-Christian philosophy as understood by Shestov. He did not, of course, deny that the principle of non-contradiction possesses pragmatic value. It was the ascription to logical principles of absolute validity that he called in question. He did not doubt their relative value.

The divine omnipotence, according to Shestov, extends to history. That is to say, God, as omnipotent, could bring it about that what has actually happened did not happen. Shestov did not claim simply, for

25. *Ibid.*, p. 302

26. *Ibid.*

27. In the third part of *AJ* Shestov discusses Gilson's work *The Spirit of Medieval Philosophy*. Gilson recognized two main sources of medieval thought, the Judaeo-Christian tradition and Greek philosophy. Shestov opposed rather than united these two sources.

example, that God could have prevented William the Conqueror from invading England in 1066, perhaps by causing William to become mortally ill or by arousing a storm to destroy all his boats. He claimed that God could cancel out what actually happened in 1066, making it not to have happened. In making this claim Shestov was allying himself with the medieval theologian St Peter Damian (1007–72). Peter Damian's view was rejected by other medieval thinkers on the ground that it was self-contradictory to talk about making what did happen not to have happened. In their view such talk was nonsensical, and to say that God could act in such a manner was to make an unintelligible claim. But this line of argument would not bother Shestov. For he refused to admit that any limits whatsoever could be set to the divine power by the human mind.

Shestov was not simply being provocative or indulging playfully in mental acrobatics. He meant what he said. The God of the philosophers, well represented, for Shestov, by the Deity of Spinoza, was clearly not a God to whom it made any sense to pray. Spinoza's God could do nothing for man. Both God and man were caught in the iron grip of necessity. The biblical God, however, could help and save even when it seemed that no help was possible and that salvation was unattainable. God could, for example, blot out one's sinful past and make it as if it had never been.

VI

Shestov's attack on the idea of eternal and necessary truths was not confined to logical principles. To borrow a phrase from Nietzsche, he was prepared to claim that God stands 'beyond good and evil'. He did not mean to imply that God is or can be evil; he meant that God himself is the source of the moral law. That is to say, there are no moral principles or laws which exist independently of God and which he is bound to accept. Shestov sympathized with William of Occam's contention that though God has in fact promulgated a certain moral law, he could, by his 'absolute power', have issued different commands and prohibitions. Occam, however, would add a proviso, namely that the principle of non-contradiction were not infringed, whereas Shestov, as we have noted, would not subscribe to this qualification.

In other words, Shestov rejected the idea of an autonomous ethics. In his view, this idea was incompatible with biblical revelation. It may be that 'we, enlightened men, put all our trust in autonomous ethics',[28] but the God of the Bible is 'the source of all rules and all laws just as he is master of the Sabbath'.[29] Moses did not either invent or discover in some world of their own the Ten Commandments; he received them from God on Mount Sinai. And what God has promulgated, he can also suspend. When Shestov came to read Kierkegaard (on the advice of Edmund Husserl, of all people), he naturally found himself in agreement with the Danish writer's idea of the suspension of the ethical. As Kierkegaard put it, if ethics were supreme, Abraham, in proposing to kill his son Isaac, would be lost. To be sure, he was doing what God had told him to do. But if ethics is supreme and autonomous, God has no right to infringe its precepts or to encourage a human being to do so. Abraham is justified only if God's will is the source of moral precepts and prohibitions.

VII

From one point of view, flight from the constraint of alleged necessary truths, whether logical or ethical, is a flight from the universal. As Shestov reminded his readers, from Greek times philosophy was conceived as concerned with the universal. Philosophical reasoning deals with concepts, and concepts are universal. Universal moral precepts are formulated by reason, and they clearly possess a value for life. But there is a higher sphere than that of reason, namely that of religious faith. According to Kierkegaard, if the ethical as such is the universal, and if the universal is supreme, Abraham, in preparing to kill his son, was guilty of grave sin. If, however, Abraham is rightly venerated as a man of faith, the universal cannot be supreme. Abraham can be justified only if there can be a direct relationship of the individual to God, in which the universal precept is transcended. At the same time, in the biblical story it was at the command of God, not in virtue of some private whim or perverse passion, that the patriarch was

28. *AJ*, p. 59
29. *Ibid.*, p. 340

prepared to sacrifice his son. Neither Kierkegaard nor Shestov after him intended to encourage people to play fast and loose with moral precepts. It was a question of maintaining that there are no universal principles or laws which are above God and to which the divine will is obliged to conform.

Shestov's flight from the universal is exemplified in a rather different way in some remarks which he made about beauty. Referring to the question 'what is beauty?', he admitted that one may easily think it only natural and proper to look for the essence of beauty. For if Alcibiades and Helen of Troy were both beautiful, and if a sonata, a picture, a view, a piece of old furniture can all be described as beautiful, must there not be some common factor, some common characteristic, in virtue of which beauty is predicated of all these objects? It is natural enough to think so. But Shestov had a different opinion. 'What we hold for the 'source' is in its nature no source but a deceptive will-o'-the-wisp.'[30] The only factor which is common to such situations is the pleasure given by contemplation of the objects in question. Helen of Troy and the ocean, for example, are quite different from one another as objects, but it is possible to derive a similar aesthetic pleasure from contemplating them. 'The pleasure given by contemplation of the beautiful is the only 'common factor', but it does not lie in the beautiful objects.'[31] In other words, objects which cause a certain kind of reaction are described as beautiful. A philosopher of aesthetics may aim at unveiling the essence of beauty, but, in Shestov's opinion, all that he succeeds in doing is to make a series of commonplace remarks. For all that is worth discovering lies there plainly before our eyes; it does not require to be unveiled or revealed by any philosopher.

If Shestov's comments about the idea of beauty manifest a certain, perhaps rather unexpected, down-to-earthness, hard-headedness or common sense, much the same might be said about the way in which he emphasizes the personal element involved in the creation of philosophical systems. In his view, to depict the succession of systems as the product of impersonal and universal Reason, operating in and through individual human beings, is equivalent to telling a fairy story. Nor are

30. *JB*, p. 194

31. *Ibid.*, p. 195

philosophies so many photographs of objective reality. 'The root of all our philosophies lies, not in our objective observations, but in the demands of our own heart, in the subjective, moral *will*'.[32] Though philosophers have indeed been accustomed to maintain that truth is universal, the same for all, they in fact 'value their own personal convictions much more highly than universally valid truth'.[33]

It would be a mistake to suppose that Shestov holds this characteristic against philosophy, as though it were something thoroughly disreputable. In his opinion, Spinoza's confidence that he was engaged in expounding not the 'best' philosophy but the only true one, possessing universal validity, was certainly unfounded, not because Spinoza was an incompetent thinker (which was clearly not the case) but because the goal was incapable of being attained. There simply could not be any universally valid and perennially true philosophical system. Kierkegaard had blamed the philosophers for not living in the categories in which they thought (not living according to their philosophies). Shestov, however, suggested that it might be preferable to reproach them 'for not having the courage to think in the categories in which they lived'.[34] As people live in different categories, in the sense that they have different aims and goals, different moral convictions and world-views, thinking in the categories in which one lives would result in a continued pluralism in philosophy; and this is a prospect which Shestov welcomed. 'It cannot be otherwise, nor should it be. The interest of mankind is not to put an end to the variety of philosophic doctrines but to allow this perfectly natural phenomenon wide and deep development.'[35]

Shestov was, of course, perfectly well aware that philosophy has aspired to become the science of sciences, formulating the most basic, universal and necessary truths. What he denied was not the occurrence of this aspiration but the possibility of its realization. This being the case, he judged it foolish to deplore philosophical pluralism. For one

32. *ATP*, p. 60

33. *Ibid.*, p. 228

34. *AJ*, p. 229

35. *ATP*, p. 228

thing, pluralism will continue to exist, whatever anyone may say or wish. For another thing, it is through this pluralism that philosophy manifests its nature as wrestling with problems which are of importance for life but for which reason cannot provide solutions which put an end to all doubt. Philosophy should try to keep alive, not to stifle, our sense of the problematic and mysterious. There is then room for the religious faith, to which Shestov attached such great value.

VIII

Berdyaev wrote that 'for Lev Shestov human tragedy, the terrors and sufferings of human life, the experience of hopelessness were the source of philosophy'.[36] If we bear these words in mind, there is obviously no difficulty in understanding the attraction felt by Shestov for thinkers such as Dostoevsky, Pascal, Nietzsche and, though it was late in life when he came to read him, Kierkegaard. We must add Martin Luther, some of whose famous utterances on faith were repeatedly quoted by the Russian philosopher. Shestov's spiritual affinity with such writers, however, did not prevent him from admiring some philosophers whose approaches and lines of thought were very different from his own. For example, his frequent references to Spinoza show clearly enough his respect for the great 'rationalist'. Again, he made no attempt to belittle the intellectual abilities of the leading German idealists, while in an essay on Husserl he described him as 'a great, a very great philosopher of the modern period'.[37] Obviously, those whom Shestov spent time attacking he considered worth attacking. And it seems clear to me that he experienced an attraction to Spinoza, though in this case, of course, the attraction was treated as a dangerous temptation.

It hardly needs to be said that Shestov found much to delight him in Dostoevsky's *Notes from Underground*. If, he said, one is looking for a critique of pure reason, one would do better to turn to Dostoevsky rather than to Kant. For what Kant called a critique of pure reason was more of an apology or defence than a critique, whereas the great Russian novelist, who had no philosophical training at all, understood

36. *SR*, p. 1
37. *Ibid.*, p. 293

where the fundamental problem of philosophy lay. It was the Man from Underground, in his revolt against all alleged eternal and necessary truths, who discerned the fact that 'truth and scientific knowledge cannot be reconciled'.[38] To reach the truth one has to abandon the so-called certainties of reason.

Another feature of Dostoevsky's thought which aroused a profound sympathy in Shestov's mind was the novelist's attitude to suffering. Though the famous Russian literary critic Vissarion Belinsky had tried for a while to accept Hegel's doctrine of reconciliation with reality (on the ground that what is rational is real and what is real is rational), he soon repudiated any such reconciliation. How could one decently reconcile oneself to the existence of so much evil in the world, the sufferings of so many innocent men, women and children? Dostoevsky shared this attitude with Belinsky and gave a memorable expression to it in the reflections of Ivan Karamazov about the suffering of a tortured child. Shestov allied himself with Belinsky and Dostoevsky as against the attitude shown by Hegel. He saw, as Belinsky had before him, that Hegel's stance expressed an exaltation of the universal at the expense of the particular. Hegel regarded human history as a dialectical advance, as the progressive self-manifestation of the absolute Idea. If in the course of this advance many an innocent flower perished by the roadside, this was just the price which had to be paid for the triumph of universal reason. This point of view was quite unacceptable to Shestov, just as it had been to Belinsky and Dostoevsky. As far as Shestov was concerned, it was exactly the sort of idea which might be expected from western philosophy which had, for the most part, laid emphasis on the universal as the object of knowledge.

In view of Shestov's affinity with writers such as Dostoevsky and Kierkegaard, it may be asked whether he should not be classified as an existentialist. The question is not perhaps quite so easy to answer as might appear. For the word 'existentialism' has been used to cover a number of rather different lines of thought, with the result that most of those who were described as leading existentialists eventually repudiated the label. In other words, it is difficult to define existentialism.

38. *JB*, p. 65

However, some remarks on Shestov's understanding of and attitude to existentialism are certainly appropriate.

Referring to Kierkegaard, Shestov remarked that the Danish thinker 'called his philosophy existential—this means: he thought in order to live and did not live in order to think. And in this lies his distinction from professional philosophers ....'.[39] Kierkegaard was conceived by Shestov, doubtless rightly, as having philosophized his own experience, his 'stages on life's way' being stages through which he himself had passed or, in the case of religious faith, which he hoped to attain and hold onto. A similar basic attitude was ascribed to Nietzsche. 'Kierkegaard and Nietzsche themselves persistently and invariably connect their philosophy not with the general mood of their epoch but with the conditions of their personal existence'.[40] In this last remark there is a hit at Hegel's claim that philosophy is its own time or epoch expressed in thought. Shestov lays emphasis on the personal element which finds expression in philosophical thought. The relevant idea of existentialism in Shestov's mind is evidently a broad one, in the sense that it can be applied to thinkers as diverse as Dostoevsky, Kierkegaard, Nietzsche, Unamuno and Shestov himself.

In addition to this fairly wide-reaching but by no means uncommon or purely idiosyncratic concept of the nature of existentialist thought, Shestov also operated with a narrower or more restricted concept. Thus, in his book on Kierkegaard, Shestov says that existential philosophy 'in contrast to theoretical philosophy is a philosophy of biblical revelation'.[41] Again, existential philosophy is 'the struggle of faith with reason over the possible or, rather, the impossible'.[42] Existential thought breaks through the barriers erected by reason in order to 'reach the freedom in which the impossible becomes reality'.[43] Clearly, existential thinking, if considered as a philosophy of biblical revelation, cannot be attributed to Nietzsche, still less to Sartre. But it

39. *SR*, p. 204

40. *Ibid.*, p. 180

41. *Kierkegaard and the Existential Philosophy*, translated by Elinor Hewitt, p. 286 (Athens, Ohio, 1969).

42. *Ibid.*, p. 309

43. *Ibid.*, p. 289

was the kind of existentialism which Shestov came to embrace. For him,
it was only in and through biblical faith that the reign of necessity could
be effectively overcome. 'For God there is neither a law of contradiction
nor a law of sufficient basis'.[44] The God in question is, of course, the
God of the Bible. Shestov felt at one with Kierkegaard in the latter's
'mad flight from the god of the philosophers to the God of Abraham,
the God of Isaac, the God of Jacob'.[45]

IX

Though Shestov wrote with enthusiasm about the thinkers whom he
regarded as leading rebels against the reign of necessity, he was none
the less inclined to accuse them of being unwilling to pursue their
chosen path to the end. For example, although Nietzsche is depicted by
Shestov as having raised a hammer against the throne of necessity and
of having looked on destruction of this monster as his life's task, he is
also blamed for having allowed himself to be finally seduced by
necessity. Thus Shestov quotes Nietzsche's statement in *Ecce Homo*
that the necessary does not offend him, as *amor fati* (love of fate) is his
(Nietzsche's) innermost nature. Shestov interprets this statement as
implying that the German thinker has become in the end necessity's ally
or even slave.[46]

As for Kierkegaard, Shestov reminds his readers of the Danish
writer's sorrowful admission that he could not achieve the leap of
faith,[47] and he does not hesitate to assert that 'at the last moment
Kierkegaard returns to the 'ethical'. It is only in it that he hopes to find
protection'.[48] Shestov also claims, and not without some justification,
that Kierkegaard, though given to violent and mocking attacks on
Hegel, 'nevertheless does not cease seeking everywhere the dialectical

44. *Ibid.*, p. 307. The phrase 'law of sufficient basis' is obviously a reference to
    Leibniz's law of sufficient reason.

45. *Ibid.*, p. 314

46. *AJ*, pp. 224–5

47. *SR*, p. 201

48. *AJ*, p. 241

movement, the natural development'.[49] Kierkegaard glorified the Absurd, but he could not bring himself to make a complete break with the ways of rational philosophy.

Karl Jaspers too caused Shestov some dissatisfaction. On the one hand, Jaspers had become 'one of the most eminent philosophers in Germany ... by reason of the depth, the power, the intensity and the quite exceptional sincerity of his thought'.[50] On the other hand, though Jaspers set out to philosophize in the light of what he called 'the exceptions' (thinkers such as Kierkegaard and Nietzsche), his sustained effort to philosophize involved reliance on the universal rather than on the particular and the exceptional. Indeed, 'in the end he [Jaspers] is forced to banish both Kierkegaard and Nietzsche from the realm of true philosophy'.[51]

Berdyaev too came in for some criticism. Shestov recognized the fact that it was Berdyaev who brought Russian philosophical thought to the attention of Europe 'or, perhaps, even of the world'.[52] At the same time Shestov saw in Berdyaev 'a philosopher of culture',[53] whose love of culturally and historically important achievements led him to prefer rational philosophy, as represented by, for example, Kant, to the flight to the Absurd. In Shestov's opinion, Berdyaev was a compromiser who tried to combine 'gnosis' with existential thinking and who found Kant more congenial than Job. Berdyaev's taste, we are told, was for philosophers and mystics in whom 'he does not find any striving for the impossible'.[54]

X

Whatever we may think about the justice or injustice of Shestov's comments on other philosophers, his remarks reveal clearly enough his

---

49. *Ibid.*, pp. 242–3

50. *SR*, p. 171

51. *Ibid.*, p. 200

52. *Ibid.*, p. 232

53. *Ibid.*, p. 246

54. *Ibid.*, p. 263

dislike of compromise and his demand that one should travel to the end
of the road, not faltering on the way. It is, however, precisely this
rejection of what he regarded as compromise, this pronounced tendency to extremism, which prompts one to ask whether, in his thought,
religious faith did not come to triumph over and drive out philosophy,
in spite of talk about biblical or Judaeo-Christian philosophy. It is true
that, as we have noted, he left room for radically critical philosophical
thought. But when in his later writings he opposed biblical philosophy
to rationalist philosophy, was he really trying to substitute one kind of
philosophy for another? Was he not inviting those willing to listen to
abandon speculative philosophy and to embrace biblical faith? It is
true, of course, that Shestov wrote about religious faith, and that to
write about faith is not the same thing as having and exercising faith. At
the same time it is obvious that Shestov was expressing a faith which he
had made or was doing his best to make his own, and that his aim was
not simply to comment on faith but, if possible, to arouse or preserve or
stir up faith in others. At any rate he wanted to open the eyes of his
readers to the nature of faith as he saw it, a faith which transcended
speculative philosophy, though it both left room for and encouraged
philosophical criticism of speculative philosophy.

Doubtless it is Shestov's marked tendency to extremism which gives
to his thought its power to attract attention and stimulate reflection. To
describe his writing as 'judicious', 'serene', 'balanced', 'devoted to
reconciliation and synthesis', would be patently absurd; it was not for
nothing that he drew inspiration from Dostoevsky and Nietzsche. It is
as though, in the writings of Shestov, Dostoevsky's Man from Underground has gone on to drink deeply of the religious existentialism of
Kierkegaard. Shestov is capable of exasperating, infuriating and powerfully attracting his readers, but he is not likely then to leave them
indifferent to what he is saying. Referring to Shestov, Berdyaev spoke of
'that profound shaking which characterises all the philosopher's
thought'.[55]

Berdyaev also remarked that, with his flight from the universal,
Shestov implicitly raised the problem of communicability in an acute
form. Shestov was not, indeed, unaware of this sort of problem. When

55. *Ibid.*, p. 13

he left Russia after the first world war, he went abroad and had an opportunity of studying the writings of Henri Bergson. 'I was profoundly moved' he wrote,[56] and conceived a great respect for the French philosopher. However, 'the same thing that happened to Descartes has happened to Bergson. The light of truth shone in his eyes; but he wanted to impart it to mankind, and immediately he was obliged to forget all that he had seen. Truth is not for common possession. It dissolves in smoke at the first attempt to receive it into the 'common world'.'[57] That is to say, if a man tries to expound and explain the truth which he has seen or glimpsed, to communicate it to others and to prove that it is truth, he is driven to use universal concepts, to employ common rules of inference and argument, and, in general, to pursue the path of rational philosophy. The truth which the man was trying to communicate then vanishes; it cannot be communicated in this way. The truths to which Shestov is referring are the truths by which the human being can 'live worthily'.[58] In his work *In Job's Balances*, from which the quotations in this paragraph have been taken, Shestov speaks of finding truth in great art, but his final conclusion, clearly expressed in *Athens and Jerusalem*, is that truth for life, truth as a guide to life, is grasped by religious faith. His summons is to transcend speculative philosophy in the leap of faith.

XI

In view of Shestov's insistence on the need for 'biblical philosophy', a philosophy based on divine revelation as communicated through the Scriptures, and in view of his attacks on Spinoza's claim that truth must be sought in philosophy rather than in the Scriptures, one may be inclined to conclude that he was a biblical fundamentalist. After all, he would not allow that philosophy is entitled to sit in judgment on the Scriptures, and he certainly gives the impression of having adhered to the robust Old Testament pictures of God as feeling emotions and as

56. *JB*, p. 115

57. *Ibid.*

58. *Ibid.*, p. 114

changing his mind, as against philosophical ideas of the Deity as unchanging and as transcending emotive states.

It can hardly be denied that, in his writings, Shestov provides some ground for our conceiving him as adopting what appears to human reason as a naive attitude towards the Scriptures. But though a reader might easily come to the conclusion that Shestov was prepared to defend the authority of the Bible against any objections from either philosophy or science, in point of fact he explicitly disclaimed any intention of attributing 'authority' to the Bible. 'Scripture,' he tells us, 'decisively rejects the idea of authority.'[59] He says 'the truth of revelation has only the slightest similarity to rational truth, either in its essence or in regard to its sources'.[60] Even if it is difficult to feel sure that one has interpreted these statements correctly, they hardly sound like the utterances of a staunch biblical fundamentalist.

Shestov several times referred to the *Genesis* story of the Fall as a 'legend',[61] but he certainly believed that this 'legend' conveys an important truth, namely that knowledge is the source not of life but of death, not of freedom but of slavery. Spinoza, in Shestov's view, was certainly wrong in claiming that the Bible does not contain and express truth, but the truth which is revealed in the Scriptures cannot be arrived at by defining truth as correspondence with fact and then raising questions about the statement in *Genesis* that the serpent spoke to Eve. Similarly, although Shestov doubtless believed that the biblical story of creation revealed the truth that the world and all in it depends entirely on the divine will, it by no means follows that he conceived this truth as equivalent to a set of statements which could enter into conflict with scientific hypotheses relating to the development of the universe but which were guaranteed as true by biblical authority. The Bible should not be regarded as an authority in scientific matters. The truth which it reveals is of a different kind. It is not a scientific truth. Nor is it a philosophical truth in the sense of being a conclusion of 'rational philosophy'. Revelation is described by Shestov as an awakening, a

59. *SR*, p. 41

60. *Ibid.*

61. *JB*, pp. 217–18

liberation from the chains forged by illusions to which the human being has grown accustomed[62], and which cannot be shaken off simply by human effort. Perhaps we can say that, for Shestov, revealed truth is revealed truth only to the human being who responds in faith and who commits himself or herself to the struggle to attain and preserve this faith.

The foregoing remarks are not intended to rescue Shestov from all charges of inconsistency: it would be difficult to do that with complete success. Nor should they be understood as suggesting that the Russian thinker was a Scripture exegete. He was not one, nor did he claim to be. The remarks are offered as a contribution to interpreting his assertion that the truth of revelation bears little similarity to 'rational truth'. But they also serve, of course, as an implicit admission that if Shestov's 'biblical philosophy' is philosophy, it is such only in the sense in which 'philosophy' is taken to refer to the truth required to live in accordance with the divine will, a truth which transcends what can be ascertained by scientific inquiry or metaphysical speculation.

62. *Ibid.*, p. 317

Chapter 7

Dead or alive?

The religious thinkers, aspects of whose thought have been discussed in this book, are no longer with us. It is therefore natural to ask whether their ideas are also dead. This question is, however, ambiguous. Is it being asked, for example, whether Solovyev and his spiritual heirs of the first half of the twentieth century have their present-day successors in or outside the Soviet Union, who devote their attention to developing lines of thought which were expressed by thinkers such as Berdyaev, Frank, N.O. Lossky, S. Bulgakov or Shestov? Or is it being asked whether the ideas of Solovyev and his spiritual heirs are dead in the sense that they have nothing and can have nothing of real significance to say to a contemporary Russian (or anyone else) who is searching for truth and is not interested simply in the history of ideas?

The first question is one of fact. Are there or are there not any Russian thinkers living and writing today who can reasonably be described as successors of the writers mentioned in this volume, in the sense that the living thinkers have learned from or been inspired by their dead predecessors and are engaged in developing or defending lines of thought derived from these predecessors? The second question, however, demands the passing of value-judgments which are certainly not indisputable. For example, while a good many people would doubtless be prepared to claim that Sophiological speculation can play no useful role in modern philosophical thought, some would disagree. Again, whereas some thinkers would argue that there cannot be any kind of philosophy other than 'rational philosophy' and that the concept of 'biblical philosophy' or 'Judaeo-Christian philosophy' is simply not viable, there are doubtless Jewish and Christian thinkers who would strongly sympathize with the general line of thought expressed by Shestov and who would certainly not be prepared to consign it to the grave.

There is a sense in which the second question can be regarded as dependent on the first. For if we were to find that there are today a number of Russian thinkers who are actively engaged in developing lines of thought proposed by Solovyev and his spiritual heirs and using these lines of thought in sustained attempts to solve problems which have meaning for human beings today, the presumption would be, or it might reasonably be argued, that the ideas of Solovyev are certainly not dead and buried, even if their appeal is felt primarily by readers of Russian origin. If, however, we were to find that we had to give a negative answer to the first question and admit that, though there are Russian philosophers, there are no Russian philosophers who can reasonably be described as successors to Solovyev and his heirs, the question would arise whether this state of affairs did not suggest that the philosophizing of the Russian religious thinkers of the first half of the twentieth century was dead and could have little more than historical interest for educated people today, whether Russians or not.

Obviously, the situation is somewhat more complex than the foregoing remarks may suggest. For example, it might very well be argued that Solovyev and his spiritual successors set out to meet a real need, a need which is still with us and still real, but that their philosophizing had features which date it and which tend to make it seem, in the case of some Russian thinkers more than others, quaint and old-fashioned and without much, if any, regard for recent developments in philosophical thought. In some respects it may have been left behind and can be consigned to history, while in other respects it may still possess profound relevance for those, whether Russian or otherwise, who are prepared to reflect on it with open minds.

Let us, however, leave this line of thought for later consideration and turn our attention to the factual question mentioned above.

II

It should hardly need saying that evidence for a growing interest in religion in some circles in the Soviet Union is not the same thing as evidence for a continuation or a revival of the philosophizing of

Solovyev and his spiritual heirs. After all, it is quite possible to experience a need for a religious dimension in life and to turn to religious belief and practice in the hope of meeting this need, without even conceiving the idea that the development of religiously oriented philosophical thought would be desirable, let alone undertaking to contribute to this development. A religious movement is not the same thing as religiously inspired philosophizing. It would be misleading to speak, for example, of the Wesleyan movement in eighteenth-century England as a development of religious philosophy. In passing we can also make the even more obvious remark that a growing interest in preserving and restoring old churches and icons and a benevolent attitude to the preservation of, say, the Orthodox Easter ceremonies as a link with the past are not quite the same thing as taking a serious and actively creative interest in the renewal of Russian religious philosophy as associated with the names of Solovyev and some of the thinkers expelled from their homeland in 1922.

One possible retort is that, although a turning to religious belief and worship or prayer is clearly not the same thing as developing religiously oriented philosophy, the first may very well provide a basis or point of departure for the second. Did not the philosophizing of Solovyev and his successors presuppose religious faith? A religious interest is not the same thing as religiously oriented philosophical thought; but without the first the second would not come into existence. The survival and to some extent resurgence of religion in the Soviet Union may very well provide the soil in which religiously oriented philosophy can grow and develop.

True enough, but we are concerned here with a question of fact rather than with one of possibility. With some Russian intellectuals we can, indeed, find a clearly expressed recognition of a need for a philosophy which 'will combine and correct all that is fruitful in scientific socialism, the natural sciences and religious (Christian) consciousness'[1] Further, it would certainly be an exaggeration to claim that interest in the religiously oriented thought of Vladimir Solovyev and in

---

1. From an article by A. Bechmetiev, written in 1969 and entitled 'From a Philosophical Diary', as printed in *Samizdat Register 2. Voices of the Socialist Opposition in the Soviet Union*, edited by Roy Medvedev, p. 159 (London, 1981).

the theological and philosophical ideas of his successors in the first half of the twentieth century is completely non-existent in the Soviet Union. Needless to say, the mass of the population neither knows nor cares about Solovyev and his spiritual heirs. But there are none the less individuals who do know and care. In an article a modern Russian philosopher (now living abroad), Dr Alexander Piatigorsky, refers to several examples of interest in religiously oriented thought, examples, that is say, of which he had personal knowledge. He mentions, for instance, a lecturer on electronics who, from 1949 until 1971, conducted a private seminar in his apartment on 'Plato, Hegel, Christianity and our life'.[2] He also recalls to mind an artist who for a considerable period conducted a seminar in which Godmanhood was discussed. Reference is also made to a lecturer who, in his official capacity, would expound dialectical materialism in the morning and then, later in the day, give another talk at home on the illusory character of material being. Dr Piatigorsky also relates how he was invited by the trade-union committee of an aircraft-building institute to talk to them about Buddhism (to which he feels strongly attracted), with the special request that he would not confine himself to giving the 'official views', of which they were sick and tired. There are other Russians, of course, who have emigrated and who have drawn attention to similar examples of an interest in religious and metaphysical themes; and the present writer has heard of one or two cases from foreign students who studied in a Soviet university. Although such cases clearly bear witness to recognition of a need, the need to fill what Dr Piatigorsky has called 'the ideological vacuum which became evident by the end of the 1950s'[3], this is not quite the same thing as actually filling the vacuum by developing a religious world-view to match those worked out by thinkers such as Solovyev, S.L. Frank and N.O. Lossky or by carrying further Berdyaev's Christian humanism. It may be said, and quite rightly of course, that no state publishing house in the Soviet Union

2. Quoted from 'Remarks on the "Metaphysical Situation"' by Alexander Piatigorsky, as printed in *Kontinent, I: The Alternative Voice of Russia and Eastern Europe*, p. 52 (London, 1976).

3. Quoted from the text of an interview with Dr. Alexander Piatigorsky, on 'Buddhism in the USSR', as printed in *Religion in Communist Lands*, vol. 6, no. I (Spring, 1978), p. 13

would accept for publication a work devoted to expounding and defending religiously oriented philosophy, and that clandestine circulation would hardly be an ideal way of 'publishing' the sort of writings in question. But if one looks among Russians outside the Soviet Union for successors to Solovyev and his now deceased spiritual heirs, are there any names which immediately spring to mind?—provided, that is to say, one passes over well-known figures who are primarily novelists or poets and whom one would not normally describe as philosophers, still less as theologians.

Perhaps my point can be made somewhat clearer in the following way. In the second chapter of this book reference was made to *Vekhi*, the symposium published in 1909, and to its 1918 successor *Iz glubiny* or *De Profundis*, in which the revolution of October 1917 was represented as a cultural and spiritual disaster. In 1974 a volume of essays entitled *Iz-pod glub* (English translation: *From under the Rubble*) was published at Paris under the editorship of Alexander Solzhenitsyn. Whereas the contributors to the 1909 and 1918 volumes had included several religious philosophers of note, none of the contributors to the 1974 book were professional philosophers. Besides Solzhenitsyn himself, who contributed three of the essays, the writers included a cyberneticist, an art historian, an historian and a mathematician[4]. This is not at all suprising, of course. In 1909 there was obviously no hindrance to professional philosophers expounding religiously oriented philosophy, if they wished. Even in 1918 Berdyaev was still lecturing in Moscow. But *From under the Rubble* was the product of the dissident movement within the Soviet Union, and by the time it appeared in Paris all philosophical teaching in the Soviet Union had long been in the hands of people who professed adherence to Marxism-Leninism with its dogmatic atheism. It may well be that this profession could not always be taken very seriously. Thus Leonid Plyusch, the Ukrainian dissident, relates that, though during his years in the Soviet Union he knew of philosophers of the most varied views, including religious ones, he most frequently came across 'logical positivists', who

4. Two of the contributors used pseudonyms.

regarded dialectical materialism as a 'mystical' doctrine[5]. However this may be, religious believers and people who had come to believe were clearly unlikely to take up a job, if they could avoid doing so, in which they were committed to expounding an atheistic world-view to their pupils. Life as a mathematician or a scientist of some kind would be much more congenial. But though it is natural enough that the contributors to the 1974 volume edited by Solzhenitsyn should not occupy philosophical teaching posts in the Soviet Union, it is also natural that those who recognized the need for the development of a Christian world-view (or, if preferred, of a religiously oriented philosophical synthesis) should not themselves fulfil the need to the extent of deserving to be described as successors to Solovyev and his spiritual heirs of the first half of the twentieth century.

Someone might object that, by thinking in terms of professional philosophers and large-scale philosophical syntheses, I make it very difficult, if not impossible, to find any living successors to the classical Russian religious philosophers. Igor Shafarevich, one of the contributors to *From under the Rubble*, is indeed a mathematician, but why should not his essay on 'socialism in our past and future' be regarded as a specimen of social philosophy? Again, though Vadim Borisov, another contributor, is an historian could not his essay on 'personality and national awareness' be reasonably described as philosophical? Further, as both men are concerned with the defence and promotion of a Christian view of human life and history as against a secularist and anti-religious view, can they not be justifiably seen as pursuing religiously oriented philosophical thought? True, it is possible to find fault with the essays on the ground that they are impressionistic and excessively polemical, but we should bear in mind the circumstances in which they were written. The writers were dissidents and at risk, and they were deeply concerned with the fate of their country, which they saw not from outside but from inside. May we not reasonably count some of the essayists at any rate as successors to the earlier Russian religious philosophers, in so far, that is to say, as successors could be expected to arise in the circumstances? After all, in histories of

---

5. *History's Carnival. A Dissident's Autobiography*, edited and translated by Marco Carynnyk, p. 92 (London, 1979).

philosophy in Russia it is customary to include some treatment, sometimes extended, of ideas expressed in the writings of Dostoevsky and Tolstoy. Is it not therefore rather narrow-minded to refuse the title of 'philosopher' to a writer on the ground that he is primarily a novelist or a literary critic or historian or a scientist of some kind? He may not be a 'professional philosopher', but this does not necessarily disqualify him from being regarded as a successor to thinkers whom most people at any rate would not hesitate to describe as philosophers.

Instead of embarking on a not very profitable general discussion of the legitimate use of the descriptive term 'philosopher', a discussion in which sight might only too easily be lost of the particular issue with which we are concerned, I propose to state my own point of view in a summary manner. If by successors to Solovyev and his spiritual heirs of the first half of the twentieth century, we mean philosophers who seriously and persistently endeavour to develop and present a general religiously inspired interpretation of the world and of human life and history, it is difficult to think of any such successors at the present time. If, however, we are thinking simply of writers who try to keep alive and foster the growth of what 'A.B.' in *From under the Rubble* calls the 'Christian consciousness'[6], and who have some recognizably philosophical interests, we can claim that Solovyev has his successors even today. But it is much more a question of recognizing a need and of indicating some possible and desirable lines of reflection than of producing anything on the scale of the philosophical achievements of thinkers such as Solovyev, Frank and N.O. Lossky. There are, of course, some internationally famous living Russian writers, but to describe them as 'successors' to the religious thinkers who were expelled from their homeland in 1922 would be misleading.

III

In the first section of this chapter it was stated that, if reflection on the situation today suggests that there are at present no Russian philosophers who can reasonably be regarded as having taken the place of

6. *From under the Rubble*, translated by A.M. Brock and Others, pp. 145–6 (Boston and Toronto, 1975).

the well-known Russian religious thinkers of the first half of the twentieth century, the question then arises whether the explanation of this state of affairs is that the ideas of Solovyev and his spiritual heirs are dead since they belong to a past world and retain no more than historical interest. If this is indeed the case, if the Russian religious philosophizing which received stimulus and inspiration from the thought of Solovyev can justifiably be dismissed as having no relevance to the intellectual needs of contemporary Russians or non-Russians, this obviously explains the lack of successors to Solovyev and his spiritual heirs. In my opinion, however, the situation is not as simple as this. There are various lines of thought which should be taken into consideration, and to which I wish to draw attention.

By the end of the 1950s, according to Dr Piatigorsky, 'Marxism-Leninism was by then dead and devoid of any real meaning'.[7] Some observers of the scene would regard this statement as too sweeping. In their view Marxism-Leninism retains a stronger hold on the minds of members of the Communist Party in the Soviet Union than optimists like to think. None the less, it seems to be undoubtedly true that Marxism, considered as a general world-view, has lost a great deal of its power to convince and inspire, and that often no more than lip-service is paid to it even by its professed adherents. For one thing the idea of Soviet power and pride in Soviet imperialism have tended to take the place of Marxist universalism. For another, the spread of higher education in the Soviet Union has not encouraged blind or unquestioning acceptance of an officially sponsored ideology. But as Marxism-Leninism had been declared the one safe guide in life, the more faith in it began to crumble, so much the greater and more obvious became the spiritual vacuum to which Piatigorsky and others have referred. The Party is, of course, aware of this state of affairs, but it has tried to cope with the situation in ways which they judge compatible with fidelity to Marxism, with retention of the ideology. It hardly needs saying that the Party cannot renounce the ideology which, it is claimed, gives it knowledge to guide the Soviet Union along the right road. If the Party were to renounce Marxism, its title to be the *ruling* Party would be deprived of plausibility. As long, however, as it tries to hold on to a

7. 'Buddhism in the USSR', p. 13. See note 3 above.

discredited ideology, the spiritual vacuum tends to become increasingly evident.

Though a great many Soviet citizens are doubtless primarily interested in satisfying their material needs and in improving their status and living standards—being, in spite of atheist propaganda, more a-religious than anti-religious—those observers are doubtless justified who see in the increasing spiritual vaccum the factor which is chiefly responsible for the awakening or revival of interest in religion in the mind of some Soviet citizens. Obviously, in a good many cases it is a question of turning to the belief and practice of a definite religious body, such as the Russian Orthodox Church,[8] the Baptists or, in certain republics of the Union, Islam, without, that is to say, any thought of a possible need for religiously oriented philosophical thought. But, with members of the intellectual élite, a turning towards religion can certainly be accompanied by recognition of the need for thought and reflection not only about religious belief itself but also for an explicit and developed religious interpretation of the world and of human life and history, an interpretation which would be capable of standing up to the official atheist ideology. There is then, in effect, an awareness of the need for a sustained attempt or series of attempts of realize the basic project envisaged by Kireevsky and Khomyakov and to which Solovyev and his spiritual heirs made signal contributions. An awareness of this nature clearly paves the way for the emergence of successors to the classical Russian religious philosophers, if and when circumstances become more favourable to the free expression of religiously inspired thought.

Although this possibility cannot be excluded, we should bear in mind another possibility, namely that loss of confidence in Marxism-Leninism may have the effect of disillusioning a person with philosophical world-views in general. A person may very well lose confidence in all metaphysical constructions of the human mind and all systems of philosophy, turning instead to faith. In the eyes of such a person it would not be a question of the speculative theories of thinkers

8. For a very informative treatment of the Russian Orthodox Church see *The Russian Orthodox Church: A Contemporary History* by Jane Ellis (London and Sydney, 1986).

such as Solovyev and S.L. Frank being dead, while some other speculative or metaphysical theories were alive and kicking. It would be a question of rejecting metaphysics in general as a source of the knowledge which can be a sure guide to life, and of looking instead to religious faith and divine revelation. In other words, disillusionment with the reigning ideology, Marxism-Leninism, could easily prompt some people to adopt the sort of attitude characteristic of Shestov. Mistrusting not only dialectical materialism but also the metaphysics of total-unity as presented by Vladimir Solovyev and S.L. Frank, they might turn to faith in a God who transcends human reasoning. In this case the ideas of Shestov and Kierkegaard, if they were acquainted with them, would obviously be for them both alive and vitally important, even if the metaphysics of total-unity were regarded as best forgotten.

The understandable desire to escape from a spiritual vacuum need not, however, express itself in a flight from reason to faith, faith being conceived as an embracing of the Absurd, of what contradicts reason. It might express itself, for example, in a demand for a revivified theology in the Russian Orthodox Church, for a process of thought within the area of faith, aiming, among other goals, at discerning and exhibiting the relevance of Christian beliefs to contemporary issues and problems. Anyone who adopted this point of view might maintain that Solovyev's insistence on the crying need for the development of serious thought within the area of Christian faith was of lasting validity and value, but that Solovyev himself went about his task, in large measure at least, in the wrong way, tending, that is to say, to convert the truths of faith into conclusions of metaphysics. As an example of this point of view, one might perhaps refer to the Russian Orthodox theologian George V. Florovsky (1893–1979), author of *The Ways of Russian Theology*[9] and other works.

In Florovsky's view one of the effective ways of combating the influence of militant atheism was the development of Orthodox theology, but it should be a theology which remained faithful to the traditions of the Russian Orthodox Church. Florovsky mistrusted Solovyev's metaphysics of total-unity and criticized Father Bulgakov's

---

9. This work was published at Paris by the YMCA Press in 1937. Florovsky wrote it in Russian and, as far as I am aware, there is no English translation. The Russian title is *Pyti rysskogo bogosloriya*.

Sophiological speculation. He himself looked to the Fathers of the Church, especially the Greek Fathers, and to the teaching of Gregory Palamas[10] and his followers as sources of religious truth. Of the modern Russian theologians Florovsky was certainly one of the most orthodox and traditional in his doctrinal outlook, but he did not, of course, claim that the ideas of Solovyev and his heirs were all dead, nor that they were all false and misguided, though his criticism of theories which, in his view, were incompatible with or at least threatened revealed truth and Orthodox doctrine was sharp and, in the view of some writers, unjust. Vladimir Lossky (1903–58), the son of N.O. Lossky, was another modern Russian thinker and writer who looked for inspiration to the writings of the Fathers of the Church and to the mystical teaching of Gregory Palamas.

It would be a mistake to think that a concern with the revivification of Orthodox theology must be due simply to mistrust of certain lines of metaphysical speculation, which are thought to endanger doctrinal orthodoxy, to confuse God and the world, for example. We have to bear in mind changes in ideas of the nature and functions of philosophy. If we focus our attention on the Soviet Union, we find that dialectical materialism is certainly regarded, from the official point of view at any rate, as philosophy. At the same time such emphasis is laid on science as a source and standard of truth, and on Marxism-Leninism being the true philosophy because it is the only scientific philosophy, that minds tend to be pushed in the direction of positivism and philosophy tends to become philosophy of science. If this situation does not promote enthusiastic adherence to the ontological dogmas of dialectical materialism, still less is it favourable to the revival of metaphysical systems which may seem to be more akin to poetry in prose than sources of genuine knowledge about the world. If therefore someone is looking for the saving truth or for guidance in life, it is understandable if he or she turns for enlightenment to the internal thinking, so to speak, of the Orthodox Church, to the voice of the Christian family. As for Russians living in western countries, if they are seriously interested in contemporary philosophy, they are obviously exposed to the various current ideas of what philosophy is or should be.

10. Gregory Palamas, bishop, theologian and mystic, was born at Constantinople towards the end of the thirteenth century and died at Thessalonica in 1359.

And the tendency in western philosophical circles would be to regard Solovyev and his heirs more as theologians than as philosophers, or, perhaps, to locate them somewhere in between theology and philosophy and label them 'religious thinkers'. Needless to say, many western philosophers would regard any such mixture with disfavour.

My point can be made in this way. When in conversation with a Russian emigré philosopher I referred to Russian religious philosophy, he remarked that one should not really talk about 'Russian philosophy', as there is only philosophy. It is possible, of course, to object to this comment on historical grounds. Philosophizing in Germany or in England or in Russia can very well exhibit some discernible distinguishing characteristics. Still, we can see what the Russian meant. In an article Dr Piatigorsky recalls how the Russian writer Vasily Vasilyevich Rozanov (1856–1919) once declared that literature should be literature and nothing else, a statement which implies that 'philosophy must be philosophy'.[11] It is certainly possible to argue that in the course of its history, there has been a tendency, sometimes stronger and sometimes weaker, for philosophy to become more and more itself and nothing else. True, there are different opinions about what pure philosophy is or should be, but this would not necessarily prevent people from agreeing that the attainment of a state of affairs in which philosophy was just itself and nothing else was desirable. Given this point of view, the expression of a wish that successors should arise to Solovyev and his spiritual heirs of the first half of the twentieth century would hardly be received with enthusiasm, not at any rate if the successors were conceived as holding the same ideas of the functions of philosophy as those held by their predecessors. For anyone who expressed this wish would then seem to be hankering after the resuscitation of an idea of philosophy which had been superseded.

It can obviously be objected that the point of view in question was not that of Vladimir Solovyev. Following in the footsteps of Kireevsky and Khomyakov, he rejected it as expressing what he regarded as a rationalistic and inadequate conception of philosophy. He did so

11. From an article entitled 'Philosophy or Literary Criticism', as printed in *Russian Literature and Criticism: Selected Papers from the Second World Congress for Soviet and East European Studies*, edited by Evelyn Bristol, p. 236 (Berkeley Slavic Specialties; Berkeley, California, 1982).

deliberately, not out of ignorance or by accident. While, however, this is true enough, it can be reasonably claimed that respect should be paid to those distinctions between philosophy and other disciplines which have emerged, and for good reasons, in the course of history; that Christian theology has come to be conceived, and should be conceived, as a distinct discipline; that Solovyev tended to conflate them; and that, even though the reasons why he did so are understandable, any attempt to restore to life the sort of mixture which he favoured would be a misguided or retrograde step. To concede this it is not necessary to reduce philosophy to, say, logic or to excommunicate all metaphysics. Not is it simply a question of western prejudice. These are plenty of Russian thinkers (and not all Marxists or atheists) who think it desirable to make and observe a considerably clearer distinction between philosophy and Christian theology than was made by Solovyev.

Although this line of argument may seem to be both reasonable and acceptable, it is certainly possible to approach the matter in a different way. Earlier in this book it was maintained that what Solovyev wanted was, in effect, the development and presentation of a Christian world-view, a Christian interpretation of the world and of human life and history. This was a perfectly legitimate aim, and in the course of his own attempt to present such a world-view he naturally drew on Christian doctrine in addition to pursuing what anyone would recognize as philosophical themes. What else could he do, if he wished to present a *Christian* world-view? It was not so much a question of confusing or conflating two disciplines, of muddling them up, as of drawing on two distinct sources of truth in the working out of a general synthesizing vision or interpretation of reality. So far from his enterprise being best consigned to the hands of historians and otherwise forgotten, it is arguable that his thought is still living, in the sense that development of a religiously inspired and oriented world-view is as much needed now as it was in Solovyev's time. To be sure, we have learned to adopt a rather sceptical view in regard to claims to have produced the final synthesis or the system to end all systems (a claim that Solovyev himself did not make). We are aware that we are historical beings, and that our range of vision is limited. But there is no need to make extravagant claims of the kind mentioned. It is a question of counterbalancing the natural tendency to fragmentation in man's intellectual life, a tendency to which Solovyev drew attention, by giving expression to the equally natural tendency to seek an overall view, one which can serve as a framework for life in the world. And if one attaches value to religion in general or to Christianity in particular, one has every right to encourage contributions towards the development of a Christian interpretation and evaluation of the world and of human life in its various forms. If the effort to develop such a view has to be seen as an ongoing process, this constitutes no real objection to making such an effort, to contributing to the ongoing task.

Though what has been said in the last paragraph doubtless stands in need of further refinement and qualification, it more or less expresses a point of view accepted by the present writer. But what has been said is, of course, of a general nature and does not show, for example, that particular theories discussed in preceding chapters, theories such as those of Godmanhood and of Sophia or divine Wisdom, have anything of value to offer to people today. Would a claim that such theories have a real relevance to contemporary issues enjoy any degree of plausibility? By way of conclusion it seems desirable to suggest one or two lines of thought relating to this sort of question.

IV

The third chapter of this book was devoted to the subject of philosophy of history, with reference to ideas proposed by Solovyev, Frank and Berdyaev. Those who believe that philosophy of history should now take the form only of what has been described as critical philosophy of history (considering themes such as objectivity in historiography and the nature of historical explanation) would naturally claim that speculative theories about human history considered as a totality have no place in 'philosophy', in philosophy, that is to say, as they think it has tended to become and ought to be. Even if, however, one were to adopt this point of view, it by no means follows that an interpretation of history as a whole has no place in the kind of Christian world-view envisaged by Vladimir Solovyev. It is obviously true that human history is not a finished whole and that future historical events are veiled from us. We do not have empirical knowledge of the future. But this does not alter the fact that the Christian religion involves or implies certain beliefs about the significance of history and about the future, and that these beliefs should have a place in any general Christian interpretation of the world and human existence. In other words, if Christian faith has any bearing on mankind's problems today, Christian beliefs relating to history cannot have lost all relevance. I am referring, of course, to beliefs about history which can reasonably be regarded as forming part of or as clearly implied by the Christian faith, not to beliefs which have from time to time been propagated by individual Christians, but which nobody is committed to accepting simply by the fact that he or she claims to be a Christian believer.

Someone might perhaps wish to argue along these lines. When Berdyaev gave the lectures at Moscow which formed the basis for his work *The Meaning of History*, the October revolution had already occurred, and though at the time there was still a good deal of intellectual freedom, the Bolshevik seizure of power meant the beginning of the reign of a system of ideas which included a teleological but atheistic view of human history. It is understandable therefore that to Berdyaev and other Russian religious thinkers continued proclamation of a Christian interpretation of history was a matter of great importance, one of obvious and undeniable contemporary relevance. For it offered an alternative to Marxist philosophy of history. Nowadays, however, when speculative theories of history are regarded with scant favour in non-Communist countries and when one gets the impression that in the Soviet Union there is an increasing tendency to pay little more than lip service to the idea of an inevitable advance towards realization of a terrestrial paradise, Christian-inspired interpretations of history seem to have lost much of their relevance, inasmuch as there is relatively little propagation of rival theories.

For my own part, I would find it difficult to attach much weight to this line of argument. It is doubtless true that speculative philosophies of history tend to be frowned on nowadays by both philosophers and historians. Many philosophers would tell us, for example, that we have no business to ask 'what is the goal of history?', for there is no adequate reason for thinking that it has any goal in the first place. And many ordinary people, who make no claim to being philosophers, have what is basically the same point of view. A Christian vision of history does

therefore have an opponent, a powerful one, more powerful perhaps
that a rival teleological interpretation. And if people continue to ask
themselves from time to time 'what is the point of it all?' or, if
preferred, 'is there any meaning in history, except the meanings given it
by individuals or groups (only too apt to be the bosses)?', the Christian
interpretation of history is not irrelevant to their problem, to their
wondering.

V

Any vision of human history developed in the light of Christian faith
involves and is inseparable from an interpretation of the human being
as an historical being. After all, it is a question of human history. If, for
example, it is maintained that the end or goal of history is realization of
the kingdom of God, human beings must be such that they are capable
of entering what is called the kingdom of God. To be sure, there can be
different views of what is required for this to be possible. Some
theologians would lay more emphasis on the part which the human
being is called on to play, while others would stress God's part, the
divine activity. But my point at the moment is simply that any serious
attempt to work out and present a Christian interpretation of history is
linked with some concept of the nature, potentialities and destiny or
vocation of the human being.

In the fourth chapter of this book there was some discussion of the
theory of Godmanhood as expounded by Solovyev and several of his
spiritual heirs. This concept was closely associated with belief in the
doctrine of the Incarnation. Christ was conceived as the God-man *par
excellence*, while other men and women were conceived as potential
sharers or participants in Godmanhood, inasmuch as they were made in
the image and likeness of God. The concept of Godmanhood was, as
one might put it, an extension of the idea of the Incarnation. In the first
chapter of his second Epistle St Peter tells those to whom he is writing
that they are called to share in the nature or being of God.[12] The
Fathers of the Church, and especially the Greek Fathers, emphasized
this idea, saying that God became man in order that man might become

12. *St. Peter*, II, ch. I, v 4.

God. This implied that the human being had the potentiality of coming (not simply through his own efforts alone, of course) to participate in Godmanhood. In emphasizing this concept of Godmanhood Russian religious thinkers such as Solovyev and Frank were not thinking up some new-fangled idea of their own invention. They believed themselves to be developing an idea already present in Scripture and in the teaching of the Fathers of the Church.

They were, of course, justified in believing this. Given, however, this specifically Christian origin, the theory of Godmanhood may seem to be of interest only to theologians and pious Christians, and to have little, if any, significance for anyone else. The doctrine of Godmanhood makes a number of presuppositions. Some of these only Christians can be expected to accept, while others, though doubtless acceptable to a wider circle, none the less involve definite religious beliefs, even if they are not specifically Christian in nature.

This line of argument passes over the fact that Solovyev and those of his successors who expounded the theory of Godmanhood were not concerned only with developing a Christian idea for the benefit of Christian believers. They were also very much concerned with drawing the attention of readers, whether Christians or non-Christians, to the relevance of the theory to contemporary issues and problems. They wanted to illustrate the way in which the idea of Godmanhood, with its presuppositions, had important implications in regard, for example, to philosophical anthropology and to the human being's social-political life. If, for instance, the human person is such that he or she cannot attain full stature except by coming to participate in the creative activity of a transcendent God, if, that is to say, the human being is related not only to his or her fellow human beings but also to a living reality which encompasses them all but at the same time transcends them, any account of the human being simply in terms of his or her social relations, as a member of a certain class or state, any picture of the human being as a purely this-worldly being, is an affront to the dignity of the human personality. If the doctrine of Godmanhood is true, then, as Berdyaev puts it, the human being cannot be 'completely a citizen of the world and of the state'.[13] It is not a question of belittling the human

13. *SF*, p. 37

being's social relations. The point is that the person it conceived as more than the sum of his or her social relations. The human being cannot be justifiably regarded as no more than a cell in the social organism of state or class.

It may be objected that these remarks do not prove that the theory of Godmanhood is true. But I am not concerned here with trying to prove the truth of the theory. I am concerned with pointing out that it has important implications in regard to our conception of human nature or of the nature of the person. In the 1960s there were some discussions between Christians and Marxists on the subject of humanism. Both believers and unbelievers can be concerned with man, his nature and his future. There is room for discussion, dialogue. And what I have been suggesting is that the theory of Godmanhood (whether actually given this name or not) can perfectly well make a significant contribution to such discussion, inasmuch as it has important implications—implications, that is to say, the practical importance of which can be recognized even by those who do not accept the doctrine or theory in question. In this sense the theory of Godmanhood is far from dead. As for presuppositions, rival theories too have their presuppositions. It is doubtless true that if all the necessary presuppositions of a given theory or idea are dead, in the sense that nobody accepts them any more, the theory or idea can hardly be regarded as anything but moribund. But if, for example, there are signs of a turning to religion among intellectual circles in the Soviet Union, it can hardly be claimed that the presuppositions of the doctrine of Godmanhood are all dead in the sense mentioned. The doctrine may well prove to possess real significance and importance for those who have had more than enough of materialism, positivism and cynicism.

Talk about 'the doctrine of Godmanhood' should not be understood as equivalent to a claim that the doctrine can be properly presented only in one form, the form, for example, given it by Solovyev. The basic doctrine can be presented in more than one way. According to Berdyaev, the doctrine as presented by Solovyev was given an excessively evolutionary and optimistic emphasis and was too indebted to the influence of Hegel and Schelling.[14] While Berdyaev had no intention of

14. *BE*, p. 36

denying the fact that the idea of the kingdom of God is a social concept (he affirmed it), he disliked the notion of a social 'organism' and felt uneasy with Solovyev's emphasis on the idea of a growing divine-human organism. In Solovyev's theory of Godmanhood Berdyaev saw a tendency to conceive divine activity prevailing over human freedom. That is to say, he found it difficult to reconcile belief in the human being's freedom to rebel against God with the optimistic view of the progressive realization of the kingdom of God which Solovyev held until his last years and which was strongly influenced by German idealism. True, Solovyev's view fitted in well with his metaphysics of total-unity; but, as we have seen, this was not a form of metaphysics which commended itself to Berdyaev.

While one can easily understand Berdyaev's point of view, it seems to me that Solovyev's idea of a divine-human organism was not without its advantages. Consider the idea of participation or sharing in the divine life and creative activity. Centuries ago Plato in the *Parmenides*, raised the question of how the term 'participation' (*methexis*), as used in the context of the theory of Forms or Ideas, should be understood, and the suggestion was made that it might be interpreted as meaning 'imitation' (*mimesis*). The concept of participation, whether in a Platonic Form or in the life of God, does not bear its meaning on its face, so that it is obvious to all. But the idea of participating in the life and common activities of a society is perhaps easier to understand, inasmuch as it is a familiar feature of ordinary human experience. By making this suggestion I am not engaged in an attempt to secularize the idea of sharing in the divine life by giving it a social interpretation and eliminating any specifically religious aspect, any reference to a relationship to God. My point is that, if participating in the divine life is understood in terms of sharing in a life of creative love within a society, the concept is likely to have more significance for most people than it would have otherwise. This is not to say that if the concept of sharing in the divine life is taken by itself, without reference to its social aspects, it is meaningless. It can certainly have a meaning in terms of religious experience. For Christian belief, however, to participate in the divine life is to do so as a member of the mystical Body of Christ, the society in which the Holy Spirit dwells and acts, and this aspect of the matter is emphasized by Solovyev's idea of a divine-human organism.

At the same time we should not forget Berdyaev's statement that his personalism is 'social, not individualist, is a personalism of the community'.[15] If he had not seen the goal of history as the realization of an ideal society of persons, including the departed, he would hardly have been able to claim the superiority of a Christian interpretation of history to the Marxist interpretation. It seems true to say that Berdyaev tended to conceive sharing in the divine creative activity in terms of the human being's free cooperation with God in working for the realization of the ideal goal of history, whereas Solovyev and, later, Frank, thought more in terms of 'theandric' activity, an activity which would be divine-human, common to God and the human being, an idea which suggested to Berdyaev the picture of God using the human being as an instrument. None the less, each thinker conceived the doctrine of Godmanhood as bound up with the concept of an ideal human society. Without this aspect the doctrine would probably seem to many people, whether in the Soviet Union or elsewhere, to be far removed from the problems which beset humanity.

VI

Let us turn to Sophiology. Father Sergey Bulgakov wrote of the need for overcoming secularizing tendencies in thought and for acquiring 'a sophianic perception of the world in the Wisdom of God',[16] a vision of the divine Wisdom 'spread like a canopy over our sinful though still hallowed world'.[17] It seems to me that a view of the world as manifesting divine Wisdom and of human history as having a meaning or goal determined by this Wisdom need imply no more than a belief in Sophia as a divine attribute or as identical with the Logos, the second Person of the Trinity. In other words, one can have a 'sophianic' concept of the world and of human life and history without postulating any intermediary being, called Sophia, between God and the world.

Bulgakov also claimed, of course, that Sophiology was nothing else but the full dogmatic elucidation of the doctrine of Godmanhood.[18] In

15. *Ibid.*, p. 227

16. *WG*, p. 39

17. *Ibid.*

18. *Ibid.*, p. 34

this case, if the doctrine of Godmanhood is judged to be essential to Christianity, we must presumably make a like judgement in regard to Sophiology. And if Sophia or Wisdom is conceived as a divine attribute or is appropriated, so to speak, to the Logos, the second Person of the Trinity, the judgement can hardly be rejected. In the writings of the Fathers of the Church we find the statement that God became man in order that man might become God. In other words, the elevation of the human being to participation in the life of God by grace was the aim or goal of the Incarnation of the Logos. In this case the doctrine of the Logos, identified with Sophia, would certainly form the background or framework for the concept of Godmanhood, and we could accept Bulgakov's description of Sophiology as the dogmatic elucidation of the concept of Godmanhood. But this position could be maintained without postulating any intermediary being called Sophia, mediating between God and the world. In so far as Sophiology can be considered a constituent feature of Christian belief, it can be presented without any talk about a world-soul or a fourth hypostasis, talk which is apt to give the impression that Sophiology is a form of gnosticism or theosophy.

It may be objected that, though Sophiology is a development of basic and familar Christian doctrines, it cannot be reduced to, for example, the claim that Wisdom is a divine attribute and that the world manifests this attribute. In the fifth chapter of this book[19] reference was made to Bulgakov's claim that, in Christian thought, there has been an ever-recurring struggle between a tendency to monism, on the one hand and a tendency to dualism on the other, between, that is, the tendency to conceive God as the All and to allow the world to be swallowed up in the divine being, and the tendency to think in terms of two realities, God and the world, the latter being conceived as virtually independent of the former. In Bulgakov's view, the result of this struggle or tension was that people felt themselves driven to choose either God or the world, either pantheism or atheism. Is it not true to say that Sophiology was developed as an indispensable means for transcending these sharply opposed and inadequate points of view? Was it not in fulfilment of this aim that the concept of Sophia as having two aspects, divine and created, and as mediating between God and the world, was

19. See p. 99

evolved? This theory of Wisdom as a reality with two aspects, divine and created, can surely not be subtracted from Sophiology as though it were a superfluous addition.

The contention that Sophiology, as developed by theologians such as Florensky and Bulgakov, amounts to a great deal more than the claim that Wisdom is one of the divine attributes is obviously valid. And even if Florensky liked to emphasize the relation which he saw between Sophiology and the Russian religious consciousness, it is clear that Bulgakov conceived Sophiology as required for the solution of basic theological problems, including that of the relationship between the triune God and the world. At the same time I do not think that one can justifiably disregard the lines of objection adumbrated in the course of the fifth chapter. If Sophia in her divine aspect is conceived as distinct from God, and if in her created aspect she is conceived as distinct from the world, it follows that she must be regarded as an intermediary being. And I find it difficult to see how the idea of divine creation is rendered more luminous by interposing an intermediary being between God and the world. If, however, Sophia in her divine aspect is conceived as not distinct from God and in her created aspect as not distinct from the created world, it seems to follow that God and the world are not distinct realities, at any rate if Sophia is looked on as one being with two aspects.

Objections of this kind may seem tiresome to some minds. But if Sophiology as developed by Florensky and Bulgakov gives rise to fresh problems rather than solving already existing ones, its suitability for use in the development of a Christian world-view is obviously open to question. As suggested above, the concept of Sophia or divine Wisdom can be given a meaning which would certainly qualify it for being considered a constituent feature of Christian belief. But I doubt whether Sophiology as presented by Florensky and Bulgakov really fulfils the purpose for which it was developed.

But is not Sophiology based on the Scriptures? And does it not have its roots in Russian Orthodox devotion, as manifested, for example, by ancient icons? Yes, Sophiology certainly appeals to passages in the Scriptures; but it does not necessarily follow that the relevant passages cannot be interpreted without conceiving Wisdom as a fourth hypostasis or as an intermediary being between God and the world. As for icons, even if some of Florensky's interpretation of their significance are open to question, there is obviously evidence for Russian devotion to Holy Wisdom. This fact does not, however, provide sufficient basis for asserting the truth of some particular Sophiological theory.

In *The Ways of Russian Theology* the Russian Orthodox theologian Father George Florovsky accused Father Pavel Florensky of having, in his exposition of Sophiology, omitted any proper treatment of Christology and of letting the image of Christ disappear into the background as some sort of 'obscure shade'.[20] Florovsky also found fault with Solovyev and Bulgakov for having allowed themselves to be strongly influenced by German idealism and, in Bulgakov's case, by the transcendental philosophy of Kant. In place of such contamination Florovsky demanded that Orthodox theology should return to the Fathers as one of the conditions for being able to speak usefully to people today.[21] In his polemical remarks Florovsky was writing from the point of view of a very orthodox Orthodox theologian, and it is commonly allowed, even by those who share Florovsky's reservations on the subject of Sophiology, that he was not infrequently unjust to those writers whom he criticized.[22] But I am not concerned here with questions of theological orthodoxy. I have been arguing that acceptance of the doctrine of Godmanhood does not commit one to embracing the speculative Sophiology advanced by Florensky and Bulgakov. And the reason why I have argued this position at some length is that, whereas in any renewal of Russian religious thought it would be natural enough to counter the view of man as a purely this-worldly being with what would be substantially some form of the doctrine of Godmanhood, theories about a world-soul or about some metaphysical reality mediating between God and the world would constitute a superfluous encumbrance. At the same time in any Christian world-view room would have to be found for the concept of Wisdom as a divine attribute.

20. P. 496. See note 8 above.

21. *Ibid.*, p. 520

22. For critical references to this accusation against Florensky see, for example, Robert Slesinski's *Pavel Florensky*, p. 44, note 82 and p. 125, note 13.

VII

Referring to Alexander Solzhenitsyn's view of Marxism as a western and anti-religious doctrine which distorted a healthy Russian line of thought, Andrey Sakharov has commented that 'the very classification of ideas as Western or Russian is incomprehensible to me'.[23] This seems to me to be putting the matter rather too strongly. One might object to Sakharov that it is simply a matter of historical fact that philosophical thought in different cultures and countries has tended to show characteristic features, and it certainly makes sense, from an historical point of view, to talk, for example, about differences between British and German philosophy. It hardly needs saying, however, that Sakharov did not intend to deny what are obviously historical facts. Part of what he had in mind was doubtless the conviction that ideas or theories should be assessed in terms of truth or falsity, irrespective of their country or place of origin. As everyone knows, Sakharov is a distinguished scientist, and he would doubtless claim that, though it makes sense to talk about the contributions to scientific theory and knowledge made by Russian or British or American or other scientists, the nationality of a scientist is irrelevant when it is a question of truth-claims, of assessing the truth-value of any hypothesis or theory which he proposes. As for philosophy, Sakharov's remark about Solzhenitsyn's view of Marxism should not be interpreted as implying that Marxism-Leninism is the true philosophy or world-view. What he is presumably objecting to is that, instead of assessing Marxism in terms of its own merits or demerits as a world-view, Solzhenitsyn talks as though it should be dismissed because of its western origin and its incompatibility with 'healthy' Russian thinking, perhaps even with 'Russian truth'. What Sakharov professes to find 'incomprehensible' is the idea of 'Russian truth' as distinct from 'German truth' or 'French truth', not the fact that Russians and Germans and Frenchmen may make distinct contributions to our attainment of truth or to our understanding of this or that aspect of truth. If philosophy is justifiably regarded as aiming at objective truth, it should be seen as trying to attain a goal which is

23. *Kontinent*, I, p. 22. See note 2 above.

universal in the sense that in itself it transcends all cultural, national and class barriers.

In any extended treatment of this theme one would have to consider possible ways of understanding the concept of truth, the relations between science and philosophy, and other relevant questions. But we cannot attempt anything of the kind here. Let us simply assume that the exegesis of Sakharov's remark which I have given is basically correct, even if it is over-simplified. In any case, whether correct or not, it expresses a point of view with which, if taken by itself, many people would agree. I say 'if taken by itself', because, while endorsing the point of view considered simply as such, one might wish to protest against its being used as a weapon to criticize Solzhenitsyn.

The reason why I have referred to Sakharov's remark is certainly not to be found in any hostility to Solzhenitsyn, which I am far from entertaining. The reason is that the point of view which I have ascribed to Sakharov might perhaps be employed in criticism of the whole movement of religiously oriented philosophy which was desired or demanded by Kireevsky and Khomyakov and which Solovyev and his spiritual heirs were concerned to develop. When Kireevsky and Khomyakov asserted the need for a religiously oriented philosophy which would be free from the deplorable influence of western rationalism and would remain true to the traditions of Russian Orthodoxy, were they not manifesting a belief that truth, the important and saving truth at any rate, was to be found in Holy Mother Russia? And were not Solovyev and his spiritual heirs endeavouring to develop and propagate a 'Russian truth', one conceived in the womb of Russian Orthodoxy? If this is the case, would not any attempt to resuscitate what was in effect specifically Russian philosophizing constitute a retrograde move? To be sure, one has every right to raise the question, if it interests one, whether or not, as a matter or empirical fact, there are present-day successors to Solovyev and his heirs, whether in or outside the Soviet Union. But to maintain the desirability of there being such successors would be a questionable procedure. Would it not be preferable to desire that Russia should discard any notion that she possesses the saving truth and that her philosophers would act simply as members of a world-wide company of seekers after truth, a truth which is neither eastern nor western, neither Russian nor American nor Chinese, but simply truth?

This line of argument may seem plausible, but it blurs important distinctions. For example, it is one thing to claim that a truth has been seen and best preserved in one particular place or country or by members of one particular nation or people or religious body; and it is another to claim that there is no such thing as universal truth, which is not the exclusive property of any one people or nation or group but is in principle available to all human beings. The first claim may be judged presumptuous or false, but it does not entail the second. Kireevsky, for instance, certainly believed that Russian Orthodoxy had conserved certain aspects of truth of which the West had lost sight. He may have been wrong in believing this or he may have been guilty of exaggeration and one-sidedness; but he did not claim, nor was he committed to claiming, that the truths which, in his opinion, had been lost sight of in the West but preserved in Russia were confined to Russia, in the sense that only Russians could grasp them. The notion, to be found, for example, in the writings of Dostoevsky, that Russia was called to lead the nations and impart to them the saving truth may have been groundless, but it did not imply that while Russia had her peculiar truth, the western nations had theirs. The point was that Russia, looked on by the West as backward and ignorant, was destined to communicate to the world the truth which was of real importance for life but which had been forgotten, distorted or denied by the self-satisfied thinkers of the western nations. This idea was unlikely to win widespread acceptance outside Russia, but it was clearly a question of Russia possessing and passing on the truth, not of the truth being Russian truth as distinct from western truth.

Well, it may be said, it is quite unnecessary to labour this point. No sensible person supposes that Solovyev and his successors believed either that truth was the exclusive property of the Russians or that there was no truth transcending national and cultural barriers. After all, in his *Vekhi* article, Berdyaev explicitly critized the Russian intelligentsia for belittling or disregarding the concept of objective truth. The real reason for taking a dim view of any demand for a revival of the religiously oriented thought pioneered by Kireevsky and Khomyakov, and developed by Solovyev and his spiritual heirs, is that the interests of philosophy would be much better served if the cultivation of pure philosophy, of philosophical thought for its own sake, were to take the place of what really amounts to religious apologetics. Intellectual life in the Soviet Union would be greatly benefited if philosophical study and thought were freed from subordination to social-political ends, class interests and suchlike irrelevant factors. It would be regrettable, however, if subordination to social-political ends were to be replaced by subordination to religious interests. What is required is free philosophizing, following the argument wherever it goes. If religious believers are not satisfied with the position of Shestov and think that there is need for religious apologetics, they should look to theologians to meet this need and not hanker after the resuscitation of a strange type of thinking, neither purly theological nor purely philosophical. It is to be hoped that philosophy in Russia will come of age and win autonomy, not move from one state of tutelage to another.

Without undertaking to discuss the idea of 'pure philosophy', let us admit without more ado that freedom for philosophical thought in Russia, as elsewhere, is desirable, something to be sought after or, if already attained, preserved. Freedom of thought, however, implies that if one believes that a certain line of thought would fulfil a real need, one should be free to set about trying to fulfil or to contribute to fulfilling this need. As we have seen, Kireevsky, Khomyakov and then Solovyev were convinced that there was a real need for the development of what amounted to a Christian world-view, a general interpretation of the world and of human life and history in the light of Christian faith, so that the atheistic intelligentsia would not have the field simply to itself. Anyone who attaches any value to religion in human life is likely to agree that there was such a need. But it is not simply a question of 'was'. The need for a religiously oriented interpretation of reality can be perceived now, not simply in the Soviet Union but elsewhere too. It is not a question of aspiring to curtail the liberties of 'pure philosophers'. It is a question of asserting the right of those who value religion, and who recognize the need to show what religious belief implies or may imply in regard to one's vision of the world and human life and history, to contribute as best they can to the fulfilment of this need. Given the existence of some evidence of a revival of religious interest in the Soviet Union, there is, in my opinion, a real need for the renewal of serious, unfettered religiously inspired *thought* in the Union. Obviously, in any efforts to meet this need notice would have to be taken of modern discussion of relevant topics. By 'renewal' I do not mean 'repetition'. But it is the need with which I am concerned here. And in view of the great gifts of the Russian people it seems fairly safe to assume that if circumstances permitted, successors to Solovyev and his spiritual heirs would not be lacking.

Index

Principal references to a particular thinker or theme are given in bold type: 'n' indicates that the reference is to a note.

153

DATE DUE

MAR 2 6 1997			